P9-CDW-538
A12900 696883

BAUDELAIRE ON POE

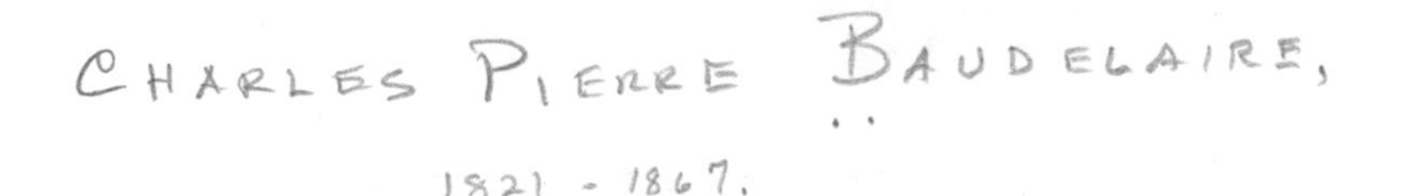

BAUDELAIRE ON POE

CRITICAL PAPERS

TRANSLATED AND EDITED BY
LOIS AND FRANCIS E. HYSLOP, JR.

BALD EAGLE PRESS
STATE COLLEGE, PA.

1952

Printed in the United States of America

DESIGNED BY ELEANORE RUBIN

for

SISSEL KATHERINE BOE

MARY MACHATTON HYSLOP

ACKNOWLEDGMENTS

We wish to thank the following persons who have assisted us in their several ways in the publication of this book: Professor Joseph J. Rubin, editor of the Bald Eagle Press, whose idea it was to bring this material together in one volume; Professor W. T. Bandy of the University of Wisconsin, an authority on Baudelaire, who was kind enough to read the introduction and to make valuable suggestions; Professor C. D. Zdanowicz; Professor L. Roudiez; Professor H. Steiner; Professor F. M. Du Mont; Professor W. L. Werner; Margaret K. Spangler and the library staff of The Pennsylvania State College. The Boston Museum of Fine Arts courteously supplied a photograph.

Among the books consulted, first and foremost stands M. Jacques Crépet's magnificent publication, *Oeuvres Complètes de Charles Baudelaire,* Paris, Louis Conard, 1922-1948, fifteen volumes. Three more volumes are scheduled to appear. Other useful works were Léon Lemonnier's two books, *Les Traducteurs d'Edgar Poe* and *Edgar Poe et la Critique Française,* both published in Paris by the *Presses Universitaires* in 1928; *Selected Critical Studies of Baudelaire* (in French, except for the introduction), edited by D. Parmée, Cambridge, Cambridge University Press, 1949; *Connaisance de Baudelaire,* by Henri Peyre, Paris, Corti, 1951; *From Baudelaire to Surrealism,* by Marcel Raymond, New York, Wittenborn and Schultz, 1950; *The Complete Works of Edgar Allan Poe,* edited by James H. Harrison, New York, Crowell, 1902, seventeen volumes; *The*

ACKNOWLEDGMENTS

Complete Poems and Stories of Edgar Allan Poe, edited by Arthur Hobson Quinn and Edward H. O'Neill, New York, Knopf, 1946, two volumes.

CONTENTS

INTRODUCTION

I

Students of Baudelaire or Poe are well aware that the translations by the French poet have made the American writer a vital part of European literary experience. So distinguished and so well known are these translations that Rémy de Gourmont believed they alone would have assured Baudelaire a place in the history of French literature.[1]

Baudelaire's critical essays on Poe, although recognized in the *Literary History of the United States* as "criticism of the finest quality,"[2] are comparatively unread in this country. Written to introduce his American contemporary to the French public, full of boundless enthusiasm and warm emotion, they reveal an acute critical perception of Poe's literary qualities, and a fervent admiration and love for one whom Baudelaire believed to be his spiritual brother.

Baudelaire himself had hoped to publish his Poe essays in a limited edition, but his hope failed to materialize. His second essay, written in 1856, was translated as the introduction to a British edition of Poe's works published in London in 1872 by Chatto and Windus. The translator, H. C. Curwen, was apparently the first person to make a small portion of Baudelaire's criticism available in English. Curwen's translation has long been out of print and suffers from a few omissions and errors. Since 1872 no other effort has been made to translate any of these three essays. This edition, suggested by the editor of the Bald Eagle Press, includes the three major essays as well as the other prefaces and notes in which Baudelaire attempted to interpret and explain Poe and his works. A study of the sources of these essays is soon to be published by Professor W. T. Bandy of the University of Wisconsin, an outstanding authority on Baudelaire.

Translations of individual stories by Poe began to appear in France almost immediately after the publication of the Wiley and Putnam edition of his work in 1845.[3] *The Gold Bug* appeared that same year in the *Revue Britannique,* a magazine which drew most of its rather varied material from British and American sources. Baudelaire's interest was first stimulated by several translations which Mme. Isabelle Meunier, an English girl and the wife of Victor Meunier, published in the socialist paper *Démocratie Pacifique. The Black Cat,* published January 27, 1847, was the first in this series.

It is interesting to note that Victor Meunier, a disciple of the socialist philosopher Fourier, was instrumental in having his wife's translations published and that these very translations were influential in persuading Baudelaire to renounce his socialist ideas and to adopt an anti-democratic attitude.

Baudelaire's correspondence with his mother and his friends makes clear how much he was impressed by the American writer to whom he was dedicated for the rest of his life. Much later, in 1860, replying to a letter of inquiry from the critic Armand Fraisse, he wrote:

> I can tell you something even more strange and almost unbelievable. In 1846 or 1847 I happened to see some stories by Edgar Poe. I experienced a peculiar emotion. His complete works not having been collected in a single edition until after his death, I patiently set about making the acquaintance of Americans living in Paris, in order to borrow copies of the magazines which Edgar Poe had edited. And then, believe me if you will, I found poems and short stories which I had conceived, but vaguely and in a confused and disorderly way, and which Poe had been able to organize and finish perfectly. Such was the origin of my enthusiasm and of my perseverance.[4]

Several things help to explain Baudelaire's enthusiasm. Poe, as an American, writing in English, appealed to Baudelaire's love of the exotic, a taste which Baudelaire shared with other French writers and artists of the nineteenth century, such as Delacroix, Ingres, Leconte de Lisle and Hérédia. Add to this Poe's preoccupation with morbid subjects which found a natural response in a poet who deliberately cultivated "sickly flowers." Further, Baudelaire's sympathy was deeply aroused by the tragic difficulties of Poe's life, which he associated with his own. In 1853 the French poet wrote to his mother: "Now do you understand why, in the midst of the frightful solitude which surrounds me, I have understood Edgar Poe's genius so well, and why I have written so well about his wretched life?"[5] Above all, formed as he was by French rationalistic traditions, Baudelaire was strongly attracted by the rationality and conscious method which were essential features of Poe's literary doctrine. In the section of his *Intimate Journals* called "My Heart Laid Bare"—a heading suggested to him by a paragraph in Poe's *Marginalia*—Baudelaire wrote: "De Maistre and Edgar Poe taught me how to think."[6] Finally, an emphasis on artistic purity in Poe's theoretical essays strengthened Baudelaire's bias in the same direction. Had Poe lived longer, their affinity of temperament probably would have brought the two men into direct contact with each other.

In order to make his study and translations of Poe as accurate as possible, Baudelaire did everything in his power to improve his knowledge of English and to gather information pertinent to his subject. His mother, who was born in England and had lived there for several years, knew a little English, but her son apparently acquired most of his knowledge of the language through his own efforts. At school he had done much better in Latin than in English. To prepare himself more fully he collected a great variety of documents, including a file of the *Southern Literary Messenger* during the period of Poe's editorship. He ordered the new editions of Poe's works from New York and London and wrote to persons who had known Poe and who might give him personal details. An undated letter among Baudelaire's papers, presumably from an American correspondent, reads as follows: "Mr. Griswold is very ill and is not expected to live. Mr. Willis is not here. Therefore I have not been able to get the information about Poe which you requested."[7]

Charles Asselineau, Baudelaire's friend and biographer, tells how the French critic sought out all kinds of English speaking persons, from British waiters, sailors and stable boys to visiting Americans, in order to clarify difficult phrases and to inform himself more directly about his subject. On one occasion he insisted on questioning an American man of letters who, seated in shirt sleeves, was trying to buy a pair of shoes. Apparently his responses were not satisfactory, since Baudelaire finally put on his hat and stalked out saying, "He's nothing but a Yankee!"[8] When he was translating the *Narrative of Arthur Gordon Pym* Baudelaire bought atlases, maps and mathematical instruments with which to check the nautical calculations, and corrected several erroneous statements in Poe without mentioning the fact in a note. While he was preparing his translation of *Eureka* he even planned to write to the German scientist Humboldt, to whom Poe had dedicated the book, in order to ask his opinion of its scientific interest.

In ways such as these Baudelaire sought to equip himself for the long and arduous task which confronted him. His first translation, *Mesmeric Revelation,* appeared in 1848, and he was to continue his work until 1865, two years before his death, when the fifth volume of his translations was finally published. Baudelaire's position in the French literary world was established by his first two volumes of translations, which preceded the publication of his most famous work, *Les Fleurs du Mal.*

II

In 1852 Baudelaire's first long essay on Poe was published in two installments in the *Revue de Paris.* Among the least known of his critical studies, it is by no means the least interesting. It was at this time that he wrote to his mother of his new interest and of the difficult conditions under which he was working:

> I have discovered an American writer who arouses in me an unbelievable sympathy, and I have written two articles on his life and works. They are written with enthusiasm; but you will doubtless find in them indications of a very extraordinary excitement. That is the result of the painful and mad life I'm leading; moreover it was written at night; sometimes working from *ten o'clock to ten o'clock.* I have to work at night in order to have a little quiet and to avoid the insufferable annoyances inflicted on me by the woman [Jeanne Duval, his mistress] with whom I am living. Sometimes I get out in order to write and I go to the library or to a reading room, or to a wine-shop, or to a café, where I am today. As a result, I am in a state of perpetual irritation. It certainly isn't possible to do long works in this way.—I had forgotten a lot of English, which made the task even more difficult. But *now I know it very well.* I think that I have finally completed it satisfactorily.[9]

These difficulties may account somewhat for the looseness of organization in Baudelaire's essay.

In the first half of this study, which is entitled *Edgar Allan Poe, His Life and Works,* Baudelaire sketches Poe's biography against the unsympathetic background of American life as he imagined it to be and defends his fellow poet against all the criticisms, personal and literary, which had been made against him. Because of the pains Baudelaire had taken, the biographical section could pass as having been written by one of Poe's personal associates, and, in spite of unavoidable errors, caused by unverifiable sources, it still remains a useful short summary. Baudelaire had no way of knowing that Poe was born in 1809, that he never went to Russia, and that apparently he had to leave college, and later his foster father, as a result of disagreements about money. That Baudelaire should have been confused about these details is not altogether surprising, since he had evidently accepted Poe's own version of his life without questioning the accuracy of all the facts. By quoting several pages from *William Wilson,* which is based on Poe's early years at school in England, Baudelaire allows his subject to help draw his own portrait. These somber pages, with the biographer's reflections on them, make a striking and characteristic passage. Baudelaire's reference to the "dark perfume" which pervades those recollections of childhood reveals the French poet's temperamental fondness for the darker aspects of things; while the phrase *parfum noir* suggests the special feeling for elusive associations which is more fully developed in his poem *Correspondances.*

In sketching Poe's biography, Baudelaire introduces some of the ideas of his American contemporary. He especially emphasizes the idea that poetry is a self-justifying activity and that direct utility should not be its aim—conceptions which were expressed by Poe in his last lectures at Richmond. In the second half of the essay Baudelaire discusses several representative works. He gives particular attention to *The Black Cat* and quotes a page in which Poe philosophizes on human malice and perversity. Poe's insistence on perversity as a primitive impulse of the human heart must indeed have struck a responsive note in Baudelaire who, like him, believed in man's perpetual inclination to do evil. He devotes three pages to the presentation of *Berenice,* a psychological horror story. In this case it is the problem of abnormal psychology, as might be expected, that holds unusual interest for him. Another quotation, several pages in length, is drawn from the *Narrative of Arthur Gordon Pym*. That the quotation is macabre in tone is not at all surprising. As Baudelaire says—and he might be speaking for himself—"the author revels in these terrible scenes . . . ." In spite of his admiration for most of Poe's works, Baudelaire is conscious of certain weaknesses and he points out what seem to him flaws in the poem *To Helen.*

In his generalizations about Poe's aims and methods, Baudelaire speaks of the American's analytical manner, his closely woven style, his salutary neglect of romantic subjects and his tendency to subordinate background to action. Above all, he praises Poe's attack on utilitarianism in poetry. In this connection it is interesting and somewhat surprising to note Baudelaire's passing judgment on Goethe whom he considers "marmoreal and anti-human," an indictment which may have sprung in part from his aversion to certain partisans of Goethe who believed that "everything beautiful is essentially useless." Elsewhere in the essay Baudelaire gives unstinting praise to Balzac, whereas he condemns De Musset and Lamartine for their lack of will power and rational method. His judgment of Balzac as one of the greatest geniuses in French literature is given no explanation, nor is one needed, although his admiration seems somewhat incompatible with his fastidious tastes. However, it is not too much to assume that Balzac's magnificent portrayal of the perversity of man, at once sordid and heroic, must have pleased and excited the author of *Les Fleurs du Mal.*

The style of the essay is not always felicitous, as when Baudelaire speaks of tears crossing the sea in order to reach the heart of Mrs. Clemm. For some tastes the tone may seem too literary; for others it will appear legitimately eloquent. Far from being distracted by his long digressions, the reader is apt to follow his reflections and asides with an attentive curiosity.

After long delays, which enabled him to increase his knowledge of English, Baudelaire published his first volume of translations in 1856 under the title *Histoires Extraordinaires*. In order to introduce French readers to a strange and unfamiliar author, he wrote an introductory essay whose composition "tormented" him considerably. It was based on the article of 1852 and has almost the same title—*Edgar Poe, His Life and Works*, although he explained to his mother with some exaggeration that "not fifty lines of the first [essay] remain."[10] It is interesting to compare the two essays. Again he acts as Poe's apologist and repeats his attack on American ideas and institutions. The most bitter remarks are reserved for Griswold, the first biographer to defame Poe. Mrs. Osgood is introduced as a new witness for the defense. Once more he draws a portrait so skillfully and so meticulously that it gives the impression of having being done from life. The biographical details are amplified by comments on Poe's moral and literary character; he gives particular stress to Poe's love of the Beautiful and to the superhuman and unearthly character of his work. On a more prosaic level he adds amusing touches, as when he speaks of Poe's financial expectations: "one of those fortunes that give character a superb certitude." Baudelaire himself had dissipated a considerable inheritance when he came of age.

Considering Poe's death as almost self-inflicted, Baudelaire introduces an apology for suicide which aroused a rather unfavorable reaction in the Parisian press. His argument in support of suicide throws an interesting light on Baudelaire's own philosophy and constitutes one of the digressions so characteristic of his critical essays. His convictions seem to spring from a heart that has itself felt the compelling need "to take leave," that has itself been sorely tempted by the "numerous company of phantoms which haunts us familiarly, and of which each member comes to praise his present repose and to pour out his persuasions."

And now to the more commonplace explanations of Poe's drunkenness, Baudelaire adds a new and somewhat unusual theory. The idea that Poe felt the need to escape a cruel and hostile environment is not particularly surprising. What is more startling is Baudelaire's theory that Poe deliberately cultivated drunkenness as a method of work, that in his drunken stupors he evoked past sensations and induced dream sequences. It is only natural for the reader to apply Baudelaire's theory to Baudelaire himself. Had the French poet likewise chosen to experiment with hashish as a method of work? Had he too found the excitement induced by drugs to be a "dangerous, but direct path" leading to those marvelous and frightening visions, those subtle conceptions which attracted him like "old acquaintances"? Baudelaire himself gives an affirmative answer to this question in his *Paradis Artificiels.*[11]

Baudelaire says very little of Poe's literary work in this essay, although he describes the general character of his contribution enthusiastically, if somewhat briefly. Poe's final lecture at Richmond, *The Poetic Principle,* is singled out for its insistence on the self-sufficient character of poetry: "it should have no object in view other than itself." He also mentions Poe's analytical virtuosity, his concern with beauty and the conditions of the beautiful, as well as his preoccupation with exceptional moral situations. In these pages Baudelaire's naturally poetic manner reaches a high pitch of intensity.

It is interesting to note that the word supernatural [*surnaturel*] occurs several times in these two essays in the sense of something which is above the level of naturalistic or realistic art. Commenting unfavorably on Courbet and other realists, Baudelaire had elsewhere used the somewhat clumsy word *anti-surnaturalistes.*[12] The poet Apollinaire used this same word *surnaturel* before he invented the word *surréaliste* in 1917.[13]

Baudelaire's third essay, *New Notes on Edgar Poe,* serves as the preface to the second volume of translations, entitled *Nouvelles Histoires Extraordinaires,* published in 1857. In 1856 Baudelaire had written to the literary critic Sainte-Beuve in the vain hope of persuading him to print a favorable article on the Poe translations. From Baudelaire's letter it is evident that he attached even more importance to this book than to the first. He explains that the first volume was intended "to catch the interest of the public" by means of "stunts, hoaxes" and the like; whereas the second volume was concerned with "a higher level of fantasy: hallucinations, mental illnesses, pure grotesque, supernaturalism [*surnaturalisme*] etc. . . . above all I shall emphasize the supernatural character of his poetry and of his stories."[14] Morally, he adds, *Ligeia* belongs to the second volume.

This essay is one of Baudelaire's most important critical studies, since for the first time he sets forth at length the principles which are to form the core of his esthetic doctrine. Having read the not altogether favorable reviews of his first volume of translations, he begins with an excoriating attack on those academic critics who considered his art and that of his American discovery as decadent. America herself, he points out, helped to disprove the theory of decadence by producing a mature and subtle writer while its literature was still young and floundering in mediocrity.

After his analysis of the idea of decadence, Baudelaire returns to a theme which had long preoccupied him: the evil which exists as a primitive, irresistible force in man. In his first essay he had allowed Poe to speak for him by quoting a page from *The Black Cat.* In this final essay Baudelaire speaks for himself and in a language that leaves no doubt of his scorn for those "humbugs and quacks" who naïvely believe man to have been born good. Like Poe, Baudelaire was contemptuous of the nineteenth century belief in progress and in man's innate goodness. The four or five pages that follow are devoted to a characteristically incisive analysis of the idea of progress and a reiteration of his charges against America. Although Baudelaire's discussion of decadence and progress allows him to express his views on subjects that were of especial interest to him, they should by no means be considered as mere digressions on his part. On the contrary, his arguments are always such that they either throw additional light on his theme or spring from the very heart of the subject itself.

It is in the analysis of Poe's literary theories, however, that the essay attains its chief significance. Its interest lies in Baudelaire's presentation of Poe's literary theory and practice, and even more in its revelation of the author's own attitude toward certain esthetic problems. Like Poe, he stresses the importance of careful, meticulous workmanship, of perfection of plan, and the avoidance of literary faults which mar the "most noble conceptions." Like Poe also, he ascribes to the imagination, "the queen of faculties," a vital role in the creation of art: imagination which is neither fantasy, nor sensibility, but rather "an almost divine faculty which perceives . . . the inner and secret relations of things, the correspondences and the analogies." These phrases seem to echo Baudelaire's famous sonnet *Correspondances:*

> Like long echoes which from a distance fuse
> In a dark and profound unity,
> Vast as the night and as the radiance of day,
> Perfumes, colors, and sounds respond to one
> another.[15]

Only through an imagination such as he describes in this essay could Baudelaire have revealed to us the hidden meaning, the inner reality of the world which surrounds us; only through an imagination which at once links and fuses our senses could he have related so skillfully a material world to a corresponding spiritual one.

Among Baudelaire's many other ideas, his definitions of poetry and of the poet are of particular interest. To him, as to Poe, "the principle of poetry is strictly and simply human aspiration toward a superior beauty, and the manifestation of this principle is in an enthusiasm, an excitement of the soul . . . ." Long poems, epic poems, are by their very nature excluded from the category of pure poetry, for the excitement of the soul, fleeting and transitory through psychological necessity, cannot be prolonged through the lengthy reading of such a poem. Utilitarian poetry—that which teaches a moral lesson—is likewise excluded from the domain of pure poetry, for poetry has no other goal than itself: "it does not have Truth as an object; it has only Itself." Baudelaire does not hesitate to criticize Victor Hugo for introducing a moralizing element into his poetry.

It follows logically then that the poet is one who possesses the "immortal instinct for the beautiful which makes us consider the earth and its spectacles as a revelation, as in correspondence with Heaven." He must have the ability to imagine, as Baudelaire has already pointed out; he must be able to seek and find the unexpected element of the strange which serves "as the indispensable condiment . . . of all beauty." Above all, he must subject his inspiration to a strict discipline, for "construction, armature, so to speak, is the most important guarantee of the mysterious life of works of the mind."

A few years later Baudelaire was to develop more fully several themes which he merely touches upon in this essay. In the *Salon de 1859*[16] he wrote at greater length on the subject of imagination and used as a chapter heading the phrase with which he here describes its importance—"The Queen of Faculties." In his essay on Constantin Guys Baudelaire included chapters entitled "The Dandy" and "In Praise of Make-Up," both of which treated more extensively ideas which he likewise suggests in this study. In addition to these specific themes, there is an evident tendency to experience and to portray the world in poetic or symbolic terms, as in the striking description of the sunset which has been considered an anticipation of the Symbolist movement.

While Baudelaire was writing this preface he complained to his mother that he was having "the devil's own time" with it, and went on to indicate why: "I have to discuss *religion* and *science;* sometimes I lack knowledge, sometimes money, or quiet, which is almost the same thing."[17] Perhaps his difficulties are reflected in some of the passages of this essay which are occasionally somewhat tortuous and rhetorical, such as the one in which he has the poet run to the east while the fireworks are going off in the west. Many other passages flash with a poetic brilliance worthy of their author.

At times Baudelaire quotes Poe directly, at other times he paraphrases him so closely that it seems almost a direct translation. Indeed, he has been accused of plagiarism; the accusation has all the more force since two years later he reprinted these passages as his own in an article on Théophile Gautier. After having saturated himself in Poe for ten years, after having associated the ideas of the American writer with his own, he apparently considered that they had become his own property. It would seem that, consciously or unconsciously, he almost identified himself with his literary counterpart. As one of his acquaintances, Champfleury, once said, "Baudelaire incarnated Poe."[18]

The year 1857 proved to be exceptionally significant for Baudelaire, since his major literary work, *Les Fleurs du Mal,* was published a few months after his second volume of translations from Poe. Like Flaubert's *Madame Bovary,* which appeared the same year, the book was condemned and the author was sentenced to a fine of three hundred francs and ordered to suppress six of the poems. It is interesting to note that Baudelaire and Flaubert held each other in high esteem and that the poet was soon to write an article in praise of the much discussed novel.

Baudelaire had planned still another essay, to be called *Last Notes on Edgar Poe,* which was to serve as a preface for his translation of the *Narrative of Arthur Gordon Pym.* Apparently he did only a few sketchy pages, since his friend Asselineau, who got these notes from Baudelaire's mother, found nothing among them which he considered worth publishing.

Over a period of years Baudelaire wrote half a dozen shorter notices as prefaces and commentaries on individual translations. All these have been included in the critical miscellany at the end of the book together with Baudelaire's first dedication to Mrs. Clemm. The introduction to *Mesmeric Revelation* tells us something of Baudelaire's taste for philosophical writers. The preface to *Berenice* states explicitly some of the subjects he believes worthy of serious attention: "mental illnesses . . . analysis of . . . eccentrics and pariahs." The note on the *Philosophy of Furniture* expresses amusement at the luxurious taste of a man who professes to believe in simplicity. To the preface introducing his prose translation of *The Raven* Baudelaire added the translation of the *Philosophy of Composition*, Poe's analysis of the methods used in writing the poem. The poem, flanked by the comments of translator and author, thus becomes a kind of triptych. These three texts were published under the title of *The Genesis of a Poem*. Once again Baudelaire is concerned with Poe's emphasis on calculated methods of work in the creation of poetry. Although it is hardly customary for an artist "to begin his composition at the end, and work on any part whenever it is convenient" in the manner suggested by Poe, this method cannot be considered completely absurd. In fact Dürer and Seurat are among those who sometimes worked in that way.[19] Charlatanism such as this, Baudelaire explains, is always permitted to genius and "like rouge on the cheeks of a naturally beautiful woman [serves as] an additional stimulus to the mind." Critics have seized upon the word charlatanism and have used it against both Baudelaire and Poe. However, Baudelaire could doubtless have developed his idea of charlatanism into an essay which would have given the word as personal a definition as that which he gave to the word dandy in a chapter of his essay on Constantin Guys.

The postscript to *Hans Pfaall* pokes fun at Poe's seriousness. It is curious among other things to note Baudelaire's use of the word *dada*. Although it has no direct connection with twentieth century Dadaism, Baudelaire could possibly be counted as an ancestor of that movement.[20]

In the original dedication to Mrs. Clemm written in

1854, Baudelaire makes it clear that Poe's stories first gave him a completely false idea of the author's life. His eulogy of Mrs. Clemm is marked by an almost embarrassing fervor. Her unselfish love and kindness could not have been more appreciated had Baudelaire himself been the object of her attention and had she been his own mother. An entry in his *Intimate Journals*, dated 1856, reads: "Write to Maria Clemm."[21] It is not known whether he wrote or whether she received any of the translations.

Finally, a manuscript note by Baudelaire, apparently intended as a foreword to a new edition reveals once more his fraternal feeling toward Poe: "In conclusion, I may say to Edgar Poe's unknown French friends that I am proud and happy to have introduced them to a new kind of beauty; and also, why should I not admit that what sustained my will was the pleasure of presenting to them a man who resembled me somewhat, in certain respects, that is to say a part of myself." This manuscript was first published in 1934 by M. Y.-G. Le Dantec in the *Cahiers Jacques Doucet* and in 1936 by M. Jacques Crépet in his edition of *Eureka.*

III

Some critics have expressed the opinion that Baudelaire's versions of the stories are superior to their American originals. In his essay, *From Poe to Valéry*, published in the fall, 1949, issue of the *Hudson Review*, T. S. Eliot has said that Baudelaire "transformed what is often a slipshod . . . English into admirable French." Of the many contemporary tributes paid to Baudelaire's ability as a translator, that of Taine is of particular interest, not only because of his eminence but also because he was a student of English literature. Baudelaire had written to him in 1865, as he had to Sainte-Beuve, in the hope of obtaining his literary support. Taine seems to have cared less for Baudelaire than for Poe, and excused himself from making any public comment. Nevertheless, in his answer to Baudelaire's letter he wrote: "what a translator you are and how well you have caught the right accent, with all its asperity, all its intensity, all its inflections!"[22] Although Taine admired Poe, he felt more reservations than did his translator. Others have felt that Baudelaire over-estimated Poe, as he over-estimated the painter Constantin Guys; and that he was as much too sentimental about his American idol as he was about himself. Yet both Poe and Guys contributed vitally to the nourishment of a great writer whose generosity in admitting his debt and in extolling the merits of others shows an extraordinary sense of unselfishness and humility.

On several occasions Baudelaire expressed the intention of translating Poe's poems, although he was well aware of the difficulties involved. A few personal comments about the poetry appear in a letter to his mother, to whom he had just sent a copy of the British edition of Poe's verse:

> I am sure that you will find marvelous things in it; except for the *Poems of His Youth* and *Scenes from Politian* which are at the end, and where some mediocrity appears, you will find nothing but the beautiful and the strange . . . . Something rather singular, which I cannot fail to notice, is the close resem-

> blance, although not especially pronounced, between my own poems and those of this man, allowing for the difference in temperament and climate.[23]

Whatever the resemblances between Poe's poems and those of Baudelaire may be, the differences are considerable and important. The French poet was not alone in seeing literary analogies between his work and that of Poe. But when someone suggested an imitative relationship he was both surprised and annoyed, as is apparent in his letter of 1864 to the art critic Théophile Thoré. In spite of appearances to the contrary, he tells Thoré that his friend Manet had not seen any pictures by Goya when it was thought he was basing himself on the style of the Spanish artist. He then adds:

> I am being accused, I, of imitating Edgar Poe: Do you know why I translated Poe so patiently? Because he was like me. The first time that I opened one of his books I was shocked and delighted to see not only subjects which I had dreamed of, but SENTENCES which I had thought and which he had written twenty years before.[24]

Actually Baudelaire translated only four of Poe's poems. Of these *The Raven,* rendered in French prose, is by far the best known. The others include the sonnet *To My Mother,* used as the dedication to *Histoires Extraordinaires; The Conqueror Worm* in *Ligeia;* and *The Haunted Palace* in *The Fall of the House of Usher.*

Inspired by Baudelaire's translations and commentaries, the Symbolists soon turned their attention to the poetry of Edgar Poe. Most outstanding among them was Stéphane Mallarmé who, as a young man, had once gone to Paris in the hope of meeting Baudelaire. One day he saw him looking at some books in a stall along the Seine, but was too shy to speak or to introduce himself. It was at about this time that Mallarmé determined to improve his English in order to read Poe in the original. Later he became an English teacher and perhaps the most successful translator of Poe's poetry. His version of *The Raven,* illustrated by his friend Manet, appeared in 1875, and 1889 he published a volume of Poe's poems in translation. When he learned that a monument was to be erected over Poe's grave in Baltimore, he sent an original poem, *Le Tombeau d'Edgar Poe,* as his tribute to the American poet.

Although Mallarmé had only the most fleeting contact with Baudelaire, he became the close personal friend of Paul Valéry, who in turn was to carry the Poe tradition into a third generation. In his essay *Situation de Baudelaire* Valéry maintains that Poe had a profound and decisive influence on the author of *Les Fleurs du Mal.*[25] In Valéry's opinion, Poe's poetic conception was the "principal agent in the modification of the ideas and the art of Baudelaire." Poe's influence on Baudelaire was unquestionably great; that this influence was decisive is doubtful.

Valéry contends that the literary analysis developed by Poe "is applicable and verifiable . . . in all the domains of literary production." He speaks sympathetically of Poe's realization of the need to achieve a "state of purity" and of Mallarmé's comparable effort to attain "perfection and poetic purity." Valéry himself seems to value Poe as highly as did either Baudelaire or Mallarmé. In an early letter to the Symbolist poet

Valéry wrote: "I prize the theories of Poe, so profound and so insidiously learned." These very theories influenced immensely both his own method and his ideas of art. Rather curiously, Valéry maintains that foreigners cannot judge the work of certain French poets like Racine and La Fontaine; at the same time he suggests that the English speaking world has not rightly judged Poe. It is clear, then, that Poe has met a need felt more strongly in France than elsewhere.

The tendency toward pure poetry which stems from Poe and was continued through three generations of French poets is by no means an isolated phenomenon. In the world of art a similar impulse toward pure painting can be noted in the period between Manet and Matisse. An artist who creates a "beautiful object" rather than a practical one or rather than a simple representational image is merely making what Baudelaire had called an "object of luxury" or a "pure work of art."

Although Poe can scarcely be held responsible for the new movement in art, there can be no doubt that he inspired a number of modern artists. Gauguin, who was acquainted with Mallarmé, painted a picture entitled *Nevermore.* The Symbolist painter Odilon Redon did a group of lithographs based on Poe. Albert Pinkham Ryder and James Ensor also drew inspiration from Poe. In our own time Paul Klee, a master of pictorial fantasy, was a reader of both Poe and Baudelaire. But perhaps most interesting of all is the fact that Manet, who was a friend of both Baudelaire and Mallarmé, did a series of lithographs to illustrate Mallarmé's translation of *The Raven.*[26] In so doing Manet gave substance to Baudelaire's conviction that the "arts aspire, if not to complement one another, at least to lend one another new energies."[27]

As early as 1853 Baudelaire's friend and publisher, Poulet-Malassis, had expressed the fear that the poet and translator might come to as miserable an end as had his American predecessor. His words proved to be strangely prophetic, for in 1866 at the age of forty-four Baudelaire suffered a stroke which left him paralyzed and aphasiac. Unlike Poe, who had died within a few days, Baudelaire continued to live for eighteen months. The tragedy was all the greater, since his mind seemed to remain relatively clear and active. Even during his last illness Baudelaire did not forget the man who had become almost a part of himself. On one occasion he showed a visitor, Jules Troubat, one of the possessions which he still prized most: an American edition of Poe. And during the last months of life that remained to him Baudelaire must have realized and found comfort in the fact that through his five volumes of translations he had accomplished one of his main objectives—to make Poe "a great man in France," greater than he was in America.[28]

L.B.H.
F.E.H., Jr.

Edgar Allan Poe

Sa Vie et Ses Ouvrages: 1852

Il y a des destinées fatales; il existe dans la littérature de chaque pays des hommes qui portent le mot GUIGNON *écrit en caractèrés mystérieux dans les plis sinueux de leurs fronts. Il y a quelque temps, on amenait devant les tribunaux un malheureux qui avait sur le front un tatouage singulier:* PAS DE CHANCE. *Il portait ainsi partout avec lui l'étiquette de sa vie, comme un livre son titre, et l'interrogatoire prouva que son existence s'était conformée à son écriteau. Dans l'histoire littéraire, il y des fortunes analogues. On dirait que l'Ange aveugle de l'expiation s'est emparé de certains hommes, et les fouette à tour de bras pour l'édification des autres. Cependant, vous parcourez attentivement leur vie, et vous leur trouvez des talents, des vertus, de la grâce. La société les frappe d'un anathème spécial, et argüe contre eux des vices de caractère que sa persécution leur a donnés. Que ne fit pas Hoffmann pour désarmer la destinée? Que n'entreprit pas Balzac pour conjurer la fortune? Hoffmann fut obligé de se faire brûler l'épine dorsale au moment tant désiré où il commençait à être à l'abri du besoin, où les libraires se*

There are destinies doomed by fate; among the writers of every country are men who bear the words *bad luck* written in mysterious characters in the sinuous folds of their foreheads. Recently there appeared in court an unfortunate man whose forehead was marked by a strange tattoo: *no luck.*[1] Thus he carried with him everywhere the label of his life, like the title of a book, and cross-examination showed that his life was in correspondence with this inscription. In literary history there are similar fortunes. One would say that the blind Angel of expiation has seized upon certain men, and whips them with all its might for the edification of others. Nevertheless, if you study their lives carefully, you will find that they possess graces, talents, virtues. Society strikes them with a special curse, and condemns in them weaknesses of character which its persecution has produced. What did not Hoffmann do to disarm destiny? What did not Balzac undertake to charm fortune? Hoffmann had to break his back just when he was beginning to be free of want, when editors were competing for his stories, when he had finally gathered together the precious library dreamed of for so long a time. Balzac had three dreams: a well published edition of all his works, the payment of his debts, and a marriage long contemplated and cherished in the back of his mind. Thanks to labors so numerous that they frighten the imagination of even the most ambitious and the most industrious, the edition was published, the debts were paid, the marriage was realized. No doubt Balzac was happy. But malicious destiny, which had allowed him to put one foot into the promised land, immediately tore him violently away from it. Balzac suffered a horrible death and one worthy of his strength.

Is there then a diabolical Providence which prepares misfortune in the cradle? A man whose somber and desolate talent arouses apprehension is thrown into hostile surroundings with *premeditation.* A tender and delicate soul, a Vauvenargues,[2] slowly puts forth sickly leaves in the coarse atmosphere of a garrison. A spirit fond of the open air and in love with wild nature struggles for a long time behind the suffocating walls of a seminary. A clownish, ironic and ultra-grotesque talent, whose laugh sometimes resembles a hiccup or a sob, finds himself caged up in a vast office full of green file cases, among men with gold-rimmed spectacles. Are there then souls destined for the altar, *consecrated,* so to speak, who are obliged to march to death and glory through never-ending self-sacrifice? Will the nightmare of *Darkness* always swallow up these rare spirits? In vain they defend themselves, they take every precaution, they are perfect in prudence. Let us seal every opening, let us double-lock the door, let us bar the windows. But we have forgotten the keyhole; the Devil has already entered.

Their own dog bites them and gives them rabies. A friend will swear that they have betrayed the king.[3]

Alfred de Vigny has written a book[4] to show that a poet has no place either in a republic or in an absolute monarchy, or in a constitutional monarchy; and no one has answered him.

The life of Edgar Poe was a painful tragedy with an ending whose horror was increased by trivial circumstances. The various documents which I have just read have convinced me that for Poe the United States was a vast cage, a great counting-house, and that throughout his life he made grim efforts to escape the influence of that antipathetic atmosphere. In one of the biographies[5] of Poe it is said that if he had been willing to normalize his genius and to apply his creative abilities in a manner more appropriate to the American soil, he could have been a money-making author; that after all, the times are not so difficult for a man of talent, that such a man can always make a living, provided that he is careful and economical, and moderate about material things. Elsewhere, a critic[6] writes shamelessly that, however fine the genius of Poe may have been, it would have been better for him to have had only talent, since talent pays off more readily than genius. In a note which we shall see shortly, written by one of his friends, it is admitted that it was difficult to employ Poe for journalistic work, and that it was necessary to pay him less than others, because he wrote in a style too much above the ordinary level. All that reminds me of the odious paternal proverb: make money, my son, honestly if you can, BUT MAKE MONEY. *What a commercial smell!* as Joseph de Maistre said in speaking about Locke.

If you talk to an American, and if you speak to him about Poe, he will admit his genius; quite willingly even, perhaps he will be proud of it, but he will end by saying in a superior tone: but as for me, I am a practical man; then, with a slightly sardonic air, he will talk to you about the great minds who do not know how to save anything; he will tell you about Poe's disorderly life, about his alcoholic breath which could have been set on fire by a candle, of his errant habits; he will tell you that Poe was an *erratic* person, a stray planet, that he shifted constantly from New York to Philadelphia, from Boston to Baltimore, from Baltimore to Richmond. And if, your heart already moved by this foretaste of a calamitous existence, you remark that Democracy has its disadvantages, that in spite of its benevolent mask of liberty it perhaps does not always allow the development of individuality, that it is often quite difficult to think and write in a country where there are twenty or thirty million rulers, that moreover *you have heard it said* that there exists in the United States a tyranny much more cruel and more inexorable than that of a monarchy, namely public opinion,—then you will see his eyes open wide and flash lightning, the slaver of indignant patriotism rise to his lips, and you will hear America, through his mouth, hurl insults at metaphysics and at Europe, her ancient mother. Americans are practical people, proud of their industrial strength, and a little jealous of the old world. They do not have time to feel sorry for a poet who could be driven insane by grief and loneliness. They are so proud of their youthful greatness, they have such a naïve faith in the omnipotence of industry, they are so sure that it will succeed in devouring the Devil, that they feel a certain pity for all these idle dreams. Forward, they say, forward, and let us forget the dead. They would gladly tread upon free and solitary souls, and would trample them underfoot with as much heedlessness as their immense railroads cut through slashed forests, and as their big ships push through the debris of a boat wrecked the day before. They are in such a hurry to succeed. Time and money are all that count.

Some time before Balzac sank into the final abyss, uttering the noble cries of a hero who still had great things to do, Edgar Poe, who resembles him in several ways, fell, stricken by a frightful death. France lost one of its greatest geniuses, and America lost a story-teller, a critic, a philosopher who was hardly made for her. Many persons here are unaware of the death of Edgar Poe, many others believed that he was a rich young gentleman, who wrote little, producing his strange and terrible creations in the midst of a smiling leisure, and who was acquainted with literary life only through a few rare and brilliant successes. The reality was just the contrary.

Poe's family was one of the most respectable in Baltimore. His grandfather was quartermaster-general in the Revolutionary War, and Lafayette held him in high esteem and affection. The last time that he visited America, he expressed his solemn gratitude to the general's widow for the services which her husband had rendered him. His great-grandfather had married a daughter of the English admiral McBride, and through him the Poe family was allied with the most illustrious families of England. Edgar's father was well educated. Having fallen violently in love with a young and beautiful actress, he ran away and married her. In order to join his destiny more closely to hers, he tried to become an actor. Neither of them had the necessary talent, and they lived in a very sorry and a very precarious way. The young wife, nevertheless, managed to succeed through her beauty and the public which she beguiled tolerated her mediocre acting. They arrived at Richmond on one of their tours, and both of them died there, within a few weeks of one another, both from the same cause: hunger, destitution, poverty.

Thus they left to chance an unfortunate little boy, hungry, homeless, friendless, whom nature, however, had endowed with a charming manner. A rich merchant of the town, Mr. Allan, was moved by pity. He was delighted by the pretty little boy and as he had no children, he adopted him.[7] Thus Edgar Poe was brought up in comfortable circumstances and was given a complete education. In 1816 he accompanied his foster parents on a journey to England, Scotland and Ireland. Before returning home, they left him with Dr. Bransby, who was the director of an important school at Stoke-Newington, near London, where he spent five years.

All those who have considered their own lives, who have often looked back in order to compare their past with their present, all those who have the habit of psychologizing about themselves, know what an immense part adolescence plays in the final nature of a man. It is then that objects sink their profound imprint into delicate and yielding minds; it is then that colors are intense, and that the senses speak a mysterious language. The character, the genius, the style of a man are formed by the apparently commonplace circumstances of his early youth. If all the men who have occupied the world's stage had noted their childhood impressions, what an excellent psychological dictionary we would possess! The color, the turn of mind of Edgar Poe make a violent contrast against the background of American literature. His compatriots consider him scarcely American, and yet he is not English. It is fortunate then, to discover in one of his stories, one which is not well known, *William Wilson*, a singular account of his life at school in Stoke-Newington. All of Edgar Poe's stories are, so to speak, biographical. The man is to be found in the work. The persons and incidents are the setting and the ornament of his memories.

> My earliest recollections of a school-life are connected with a large, rambling, Elizabethan house, in a misty-looking village of England, where were a vast number of gigantic and gnarled trees, and where all the houses were excessively ancient. In truth, it was a dream-like and spirit-soothing place, that venerable old town. At this moment, in fancy, I feel the refreshing chilliness of its deeply-shadowed avenues, inhale the fragrance of its thousand shrubberies, and thrill anew with undefinable delight, at the deep hollow note of the church-bell, breaking, each hour, with sullen and sudden roar, upon the stillness of the dusky atmosphere in which the fretted Gothic steeple lay imbedded and asleep.
>
> It gives me, perhaps, as much of pleasure as I can now in any manner experience, to dwell upon minute recollections of the school and its concerns. Steeped in misery as I am—misery, alas! only too real—I shall be pardoned for seeking relief, however slight and temporary, in the weakness of a few rambling details. These, moreover, utterly trivial, and even ridiculous in themselves, assume, to my fancy, adventitious importance, as connected with a period and a locality when and where I recognize the first ambiguous monitions of the destiny which afterward so fully overshadowed me. Let me then remember.
>
> The house, I have said, was old and irregular. The grounds were extensive, and a high and solid brick wall, topped with a bed of mortar and broken glass, encompassed the whole. This prison-like rampart formed the limit of our domain; beyond it we saw but thrice a week—once every Saturday afternoon, when, attended by two ushers, we were permit-

ted to take brief walks in a body through some of the neighboring fields—and twice during Sunday, when we were paraded in the same formal manner to the morning and evening service in the one church of the village. Of this church the principal of our school was pastor. With how deep a spirit of wonder and perplexity was I wont to regard him from our remote pew in the gallery, as, with step solemn and slow, he ascended the pulpit! This reverend man, with countenance so demurely benign, with robes so glossy and so clerically flowing, with wig so minutely powdered, so rigid and so vast,—could this be he who, of late, with sour visage, and in snuffy habiliments, administered, ferule in hand, the Draconian Laws of the academy? Oh, gigantic paradox, too utterly monstrous for solution!

At an angle of the ponderous wall frowned a more ponderous gate. It was riveted and studded with iron bolts, and surmounted with jagged iron spikes. What impressions of deep awe did it inspire! It was never opened save for the three periodical egressions and ingressions already mentioned; then, in every creak of its mighty hinges, we found a plenitude of mystery—a world of matter for solemn remark, or for more solemn meditation.

The extensive enclosure was irregular in form, having many capacious recesses. Of these, three or four of the largest constituted the playground. It was level, and covered with fine hard gravel. I well remember it had no trees, nor benches, nor any thing similar within it. Of course it was in the rear of the house. In front lay a small parterre, planted with box and other shrubs, but through this sacred division we passed only upon rare occasions indeed—such as a first advent to school or final departure thence, or perhaps, when a parent or friend having called for us, we joyfully took our way home for the Christmas or Midsummer holidays.

But the house!—how quaint an old building was this!—to me how veritable a palace of enchantment!

There was really no end to its windings—to its incomprehensible subdivisions. It was difficult, at any given time, to say with certainty upon which of its two stories one happened to be. From each room to every other there was sure to be found three or four steps either in ascent or descent. Then the lateral branches were innumerable—inconceivable—and so returning in upon themselves, that our most exact ideas in regard to the whole mansion were not very far different from those with which we pondered upon infinity. During the five years of my residence here, I was never able to ascertain with precision, in what remote locality lay the little sleeping apartment assigned to myself and some eighteen or twenty other scholars.

The school-room was the largest in the house—I could not help thinking, in the world. It was very long, narrow, and dismally low, with pointed Gothic windows and a ceiling of oak. In a remote and terror-inspiring angle was a square enclosure of eight or ten feet, comprising the *sanctum,* 'during hours,' of our principal, the Reverend Dr. Bransby. It was a solid structure, with massy door, sooner than open which in the absence of the 'Dominie,' we would all have willingly perished by the *peine forte et dure.* In other angles were two other similar boxes, far less reverenced, indeed, but still greatly matters of awe. One of these was the pulpit of the 'classical' usher, one of the 'English and mathematical.' Interspersed about the room, crossing and recrossing in endless irregularity, were innumerable benches and desks, black, ancient, and time-worn, piled desperately with much bethumbed books, and so beseamed with initial letters, names at full length, grotesque figures, and other multiplied efforts of the knife, as to have entirely lost what little of original form might have been their portion in days long departed. A huge bucket with water stood at one extremity of the room, and a clock of stupendous dimensions at the other.

Encompassed by the massy walls of this venerable

> academy, I passed, yet not in tedium or disgust, the years of the third lustrum of my life. The teeming brain of childhood requires no external world of incident to occupy or amuse it; and the apparently dismal monotony of a school was replete with more intense excitement than my riper youth has derived from luxury, or my full manhood from crime. Yet I must believe that my first mental development had in it much of the uncommon—even much of the *outré*. Upon mankind at large the events of very early existence rarely leave in mature age any definite impression. All is gray shadow—a weak and irregular remembrance—an indistinct regathering of feeble pleasures and phantasmagoric pains. With me this is not so. In childhood, I must have felt with the energy of a man what I now find stamped upon memory in lines as vivid, as deep, and as durable as the *exergues* of the Carthaginian medals.
>
> Yet in fact—in the fact of the world's view—how little was there to remember! The morning's awakening, the nightly summons to bed; the connings, the recitations; the periodical half-holidays, and perambulations; the play-ground, with its broils, its pastimes, its intrigues;—these, by a mental sorcery long forgotten, were made to involve a wilderness of sensation, a world of rich incident, an universe of varied emotion, of excitement, the most passionate and spirit-stirring. *'Oh, le bon temps, que ce siècle de fer!'*[8]

What do you think of this passage? Does not the character of this remarkable man begin to reveal itself? For my part, I feel that this picture of school life gives off a dark perfume. I sense the shiver of somber years of confinement running through it. Hours of imprisonment, the anxiety of a lonely and miserable childhood, fear of the master, our enemy, the hate of brutal comrades, the heart's solitude, all these tortures of youth

Edgar Poe somehow escapes. All those causes of melancholy fail to overcome him. Though young, he loves solitude, or rather he does not feel himself alone; he loves his own passions. *The fertile mind of childhood* makes everything agreeable, illuminates everything. Already it is clear that will power and solitary pride will play a great role in his life. Would you not say, indeed, that he is almost fond of suffering, that he has a presentiment of the inseparable companion of his future life, and that he seeks it with an eager desire, like a young gladiator? The poor child has neither father nor mother, but he is happy; he glories in being deeply stamped, *like a Carthaginian medal.*

Edgar Poe returned from Dr. Bransby's school to Richmond in 1822, and continued his studies under the best teachers. He was then a young man quite remarkable for his physical prowess, grace and suppleness, and to the attractions of a strikingly handsome appearance, he joined a marvelously powerful poetic memory and the precocious faculty of improvising stories. In 1825 he entered the University of Virginia which was at that time a center of dissipation. Edgar Poe distinguished himself among his fellow students by an exceptionally lively eagerness for pleasure. He was an excellent student and made incredible progress in mathematics; he had an unusual aptitude for physics and natural science, which may be noted in passing, since in several of his works there appears a great preoccupation with science; but at the same time he drank, gambled and behaved so wildly that he was finally expelled. When Mr. Allan refused to pay some gambling debts, he broke with him impulsively and ran away to Greece. It was the period of Botzaris and the Greek Revolution. Finally turning up in St. Petersburg, his purse and enthusiasm somewhat exhausted, he got into trouble with the Russian government for reasons unknown. It is said that the situation was so bad that Poe was about to add Siberia to his precocious knowledge of men and things.[9] Finally, the intervention and help of Henry Middleton, the American Consul, enabled him to return home. In 1829 he entered the military academy at West Point. Meanwhile, Mr. Allan, whose first wife had died, had married a woman very much younger than himself. He was then sixty-five years old. It is said that Poe behaved improperly, and that he ridiculed the marriage. The old gentleman wrote him a very severe letter, to which Poe replied with a letter even more bitter. The wound could not be healed, and shortly afterward Mr. Allan died without leaving a penny to his adopted son.

At this point in the biographical account of Edgar Allan Poe I find very mysterious statements, very strange and obscure allusions concerning the conduct of our future writer. The biographer seriously discredits Poe while maintaining most hypocritically that he prefers to say absolutely nothing, suggesting that there are things which must be always hidden (why?), that in certain shocking cases silence should take precedence over history. The attack is all the more dangerous because of its ambiguity. What the devil does he mean? Does he wish to insinuate that Poe tried to seduce his father's new wife? It is quite impossible to guess. But I believe I have said enough to put the reader on his guard about American biographers. They are too good democrats not to hate their great men, and the ill-will which pursued Poe after the lamentable end of his sad existence recalls the hatred with which the British persecuted Byron.

Poe left West Point without graduating, and began his disastrous battle with life. In 1831 he published a small volume of poems which was favorably reviewed, but which did not sell. It was the eternal story of a first book. Lowell, an American critic, said that in one of the poems entitled, *To Helen,* there was *an ambrosial perfume,* and that the poem would not mar the Greek anthology. It has to do with Nicean barques, Naiads, Greek beauty and glory, and the lamp of Psyche. In passing we may note the American tendency toward the pastiche which is characteristic of an immature literature. It is true that through its harmonious rhythm and its sonorous rimes, with five lines, two masculine and three feminine, it recalls the happy efforts of French romanticism. But it is evident that Poe was still quite far from his eccentric and meteoric literary destiny.

Meanwhile the unlucky man was writing for newspapers, doing hack work, translating, sending brilliant articles and stories to the magazines. The editors were glad to publish them, but they paid the poor young man so badly that he became frightfully impoverished. He even sank so low that for a moment he could hear *the creaking hinges of the gates of death.* One day a Baltimore paper offered two prizes, one for the best poem, the other for the best story. Mr. John Kennedy was a member of the literary jury asked to judge the compositions. The jury scarcely bothered to read them, however; the editor wanted only the sanction of their names. As they were talking about one thing and another, one of them was attracted by a manuscript which stood out because of the beauty, neatness and clearness of its handwriting. At the end of his life Edgar Poe still had an incomparably beautiful hand. (This remark strikes me as quite American.) Mr. Kennedy read one page, and struck by the style, he read the whole composition aloud. The jury awarded the prize by acclamation to the first genius who could write legibly.[10] The sealed envelope was opened and revealed the name Poe, which was then unknown.

The editor talked so enthusiastically to Mr. Kennedy about the young author that the latter wanted to meet him. Cruel fortune had given Poe the classic appearance of a starving poet. It had made him up as effectively as possible for the role. Mr. Kennedy reports that he found a young man grown as thin as a skeleton through privations, dressed in a threadbare frock-coat which was buttoned up to his chin, as is customary in such cases, wearing ragged trousers, torn boots over bare feet, and yet with all that a proud air, a grand manner, and eyes sparkling with intelligence. Kennedy talked to him in a friendly way and put him at his ease. Poe spoke frankly, told his whole story and mentioned his ambitions and his great projects. Kennedy immediately took him to a store (a second-hand clothes dealer, as Lesage would have said) and got him some suitable clothes; then he introduced him to the right people.

It was at this time that a Mr. Thomas White, who had bought the *Southern Literary Messenger*, chose Poe as editor and gave him a salary of 2,500 francs a year. Poe immediately married a young girl without a cent. (The phraseology is not mine; please notice the slight tone of scorn in that *immediately* (the poor man thought he was rich), and in the dry, laconic day in which he announces an important event; and also note the phrase, a girl without a cent!) It is said that already he was drinking too much, but the fact remains that he found time to write a very large number of articles and fine critical studies for the *Messenger*. After having directed it for a year and a half, he went to Philadelphia and edited *The Gentleman's Magazine.* When that periodical merged with *Graham's Magazine,* Poe continued to write for it. In 1840 he published *Tales of the Grotesque and Arabesque.* In 1844 we find him in New York, editing the *Broadway Journal.* In 1845 appeared the well known small volume of poems and stories, published by Wiley and Putnam. This is the edition from which the French translators have drawn almost all the examples of Edgar Poe's talent which have appeared in the journals of Paris. Up until 1847 he published a succession of different works which we shall discuss later. We learn now that his wife died in a town called Fordham, near New York, in a profund state of destitution. The literary people of New York raised a fund to help Poe. Shortly afterwards the papers again spoke of him as a man close to death. This time it was something quite serious, he had delirium tremens. A cruel note, published in a paper at this time, takes him to task for his scorn of all those who claimed to be his friends, and for his general disgust with the world. Although he was making money, and his literary work was earning nearly enough to support him, it is evident from the remarks of his biographers that he had humiliating difficulties to overcome. It appears that during his last two years, on his occasional visits to Richmond, he very much scandalized people by his drunken habits. Hearing the endless recriminations on that subject, one would suppose that all the writers in the United States are models of sobriety. But in his final visit, which lasted for nearly two months, he suddenly appeared neat, elegant, correct, charming in his manners, and as handsome as a genius. Evidently I lack some of the necessary facts, and the notes at my disposal are not sufficiently intelligible to account for these startling transformations. Perhaps they can be explained by the watchful maternal protection which shielded the somber writer, and which combatted with angelic arms the evil demon born of his blood and of his previous sufferings.

During this last visit to Richmond he gave two public lectures. A word should be said about lectures of this kind which play an important role in the literary life of the United States. Any writer, philosopher, poet, in fact anyone who can talk, may give a lecture, a public dissertation on some literary or philosophical subject. A hall is hired. Everyone pays admission in order to have the pleasure of hearing new ideas and of enjoying platform eloquence. The public comes or stays away. In the latter case, it is an unsuccessful speculation, like any other risky commercial venture. However, when the lecturer is a famous writer, the hall is crowded and the event becomes a solemn literary occasion. It is like making the *Collège de France* available to everyone. It reminds one of Andrieux, of La Harpe, of Baour-Lormian, and recalls the kind of literary restoration which took place in the Lyceums, the Athenaeums and the Casinos after the French Revolution.

Edgar Poe chose as his subject a perennially interesting theme, and one which has been heatedly discussed in this country. He announced that he would speak about the *poetic principle.* For a long time there has been a utilitarian movement in the United States which seeks to carry poetry along with it, like everything else. There are humanitarian poets, poets who favor women's suffrage, poets opposed to the tax on cereals, and poets who wish to build workhouses. I swear that I am not referring to people in France. It is not my fault if the same disputes and the same theories agitate different countries. In his lectures Poe declared war on all that. He did not maintain, as do certain mad and fanatical partisans of Goethe and other marmoreal and anti-human poets, that everything beautiful is essentially useless; but he did undertake the task of refuting what he wittily called *the great poetic heresy of modern times.* This heresy is the idea of direct utility. It can be seen that to a certain extent Edgar Poe is in agreement with French romanticism. He said: "Our mind possesses elementary faculties whose purposes differ. Some are concerned with satisfying reason, others perceive forms and colors, still others serve a constructive purpose. Logic, painting, mechanics are the results of these faculties. And just as we have nerves for sensing pleasant odors, nerves for feeling beautiful colors, and to delight us in contact with smooth surfaces, we have an elementary faculty which enables us to perceive the beautiful; it has its own purpose and its own means. Poetry is the product of this faculty; it addresses itself to the sense of the beautiful and not to any other. *To subject it to the criteria of other faculties is to damage it,* and it is never applicable to matters other than those which are necessarily the food of the intellectual organ to which it owes its birth. There can be no doubt that subsequently and consequently poetry may be useful, but that is not its purpose; that comes as something *over and above* its chief function. No one is surprised if a market, a dock or any other industrial construction satisfies the conditions of the beautiful, although that was not the principal aim and primary ambition of the engineer or architect." Poe *illustrated* his thesis by critical remarks about American poets, and by reciting some English poems. He was asked to read *The Raven.* American critics attach a great deal of importance to this poem. They speak of it as a very remarkable piece of versification, with an ample and complex rhythm, and a masterly interlacement of rimes flattering to their national pride, which is a little jealous of European *tours de force.* But it seems that the audience was disappointed by the author's reading, since he did not know how to give his work a brilliant effect. Pure delivery, but a low voice, a monotonous recitative, a rather marked disregard of the musical effects which his skillful pen had, as it were, indicated, failed to please those who had looked forward to a comparison of reader and author. I am not at all surprised by this. I have often noticed that excellent poets are deplorable performers. That often happens in the case of persons who are serious and reserved. Profound writers are not orators, and that is a good thing.

A very large audience filled the hall. All those who had not seen Edgar Poe since the days of his obscurity crowded in to see their now illustrious fellow citizen. Such an enthusiastic reception filled his poor heart with joy. He felt a very legitimate and a very pardonable pride. He was so delighted that he spoke of settling permanently in Richmond. It was rumored that he was going to re-marry. Talk centered on a widowed lady, as rich as she was beautiful, one of Poe's former passions, who was thought to have been the original model for his *Lenore*. Meanwhile he had to make a trip to New York in connection with the publication of a new edition of his stories. In addition, the husband of a wealthy woman in New York asked Poe to edit his wife's poems, write notes, a preface, etc.

Poe left Richmond; but on the way he complained of chills and weakness. Still feeling rather ill when he arrived in Baltimore, he took a drink as a stimulant. It was the first time that he had touched the accursed alcohol for several months; but that was enough to arouse the Devil sleeping within him. A drinking bout brought on another attack of *delirium tremens,* his old acquaintance. In the morning the police found him lying on the street, in a state of stupor. Since he had no money, friends or home address, they took him to the hospital, and it was there that the author of *The Black Cat* and of *Eureka,* died, on the 7th of October, 1849, at the age of 37.[11]

Edgar Poe left no relatives except a sister who lives in Richmond. His wife had died some time before him, and they had no children. She was a Miss Clemm, and was her husband's cousin. His mother-in-law was deeply attached to Poe. She was his companion through all his misfortunes, and was terribly stricken by his premature death. The bond which united their souls was not broken by the death of her daughter. A devotion so great, an affection so noble, so steadfast, does Edgar Poe great honor. Certainly he who was able to inspire such boundless love possessed virtues, and his spiritual character must have been very attractive.

Mr. Willis has published a short note about Poe; a portion of it follows:

> Our first knowledge of Mr. Poe's removal to this city was by a call which we received from a lady who introduced herself to us as the mother of his wife. She was in search of employment for him, and she excused her errand by mentioning that he was ill, that her daughter was a confirmed invalid, and that their circumstances were such as compelled her taking it upon herself. The countenance of this lady, made beautiful and saintly with an evidently complete giving up of her life to privation and sorrowful tenderness, her gentle and mournful voice urging its plea, her long-forgotten but habitually and unconsciously refined manners, and her appealing and yet appreciative mention of the claims and abilities of her son, disclosed at once the presence of one of those angels upon earth that women in adversity can be. It was a hard fate that she was watching over. Mr. Poe wrote with fastidious difficulty, and in a style too much above the popular level to be well paid. He was always in pecuniary difficulty, and, with his sick wife, frequently in want of the merest necessaries of life. Winter after winter, for years, the most touching sight to us, in this whole city, has been that tireless minister to genius, thinly and insufficiently clad, going from office to office with a poem, or an article on some literary subject, to sell, —sometimes simply pleading in a broken voice that he was ill, and begging for him,—mentioning nothing but that 'he was ill,' whatever might be the reason for his writing nothing,—and never, amid all her tears and recitals of distress, suffering one syllable to escape her lips that could convey a doubt of him,

or a complaint, or a lessening of pride in his genius and good intentions. Her daughter died a year and a half since, but she did not desert him. She continued his ministering angel—living with him, caring for him, guarding him against exposure, and, when he was carried away by temptation, amid grief and the loneliness of feelings unreplied to, and awoke from his self-abandonment prostrated in destitution and suffering, begging for him still. If woman's devotion, born with a first love and fed with human passion, hallows its object, as it is allowed to do, what does not a devotion like this—pure, disinterested, and holy as the watch of an invisible spirit—say for him who inspired it?

We have a letter before us, written by this lady, Mrs. Clemm, on the morning in which she heard of the death of this object of her untiring care. It is merely a request that we would call upon her, but we will copy a few of its words—sacred as its privacy is—to warrant the truth of the picture we have drawn above, and add force to the appeal we wish to make for her:

"I have this morning heard of the death of my darling Eddie. *** Can you give me any circumstances or particulars? *** Oh! do not desert your poor friend in this bitter affliction. *** Ask Mr. — to come, as I must deliver a message to him from my poor Eddie. *** I need not ask you to notice his death and to speak well of him. I know you will. But say what an affectionate son he was to me, his poor desolate mother.***"[12]

How much this poor woman is concerned with the reputation of her son-in-law! How beautiful! How great! Admirable woman, just as freedom is superior to fatality, just as spirit is greater than flesh, so your affection transcends all human affections! May our tears traverse the ocean, the tears of all those who, like your poor Eddie, are unfortunate, anxious, and who are led into debauchery through poverty and suffering, may these tears find their way to your heart! May these lines, stamped with the most sincere and the most respectful admiration, please your maternal eyes! Your almost divine image will hover unceasingly above the martyrology of literature!

Poe's death aroused profound emotion in America. Sincere expressions of grief appeared throughout the Union. Sometimes death causes many things to be pardoned. We are glad to mention a letter by Longfellow[13] which is all the more creditable since Poe had treated him very badly. "What a melancholy death is that of Mr. Poe—a man so richly endowed with genius! I never knew him personally, but have always entertained a high appreciation of his powers as a prose writer and a poet. His prose is remarkably vigorous, direct and yet affluent; and his verse has a peculiar charm of melody, an atmosphere of true poetry about it which is very winning. The harshness of his criticisms I have never attributed to anything but the irritation of a sensitive nature, chafed by some indefinite sense of wrong."

It is amusing to hear the prolix author of *Evangeline* speak of Poe's *affluence.* Does he consider Poe a mirror?

II

It is a very great and a very useful pleasure to compare the traits of a great man with his works. Biographies, notes on the manners, habits and physical appearance of artists and writers have always excited a very legitimate curiosity. Who has not on occasion sought the acuity of style and the clear ideas of Erasmus in the sharpness of his profile, the heat and fustian of Diderot's and Mercier's works in the appearance of their heads where good nature is mixed with a little bluster, the stubborn irony of Voltaire in his persistent smile, his combative grimace, the power of command and prophecy visible in the searching eye and in the solid figure of Joseph de Maistre,[14] at once an eagle and an ox? Who has not tried to decipher the *Human Comedy* in the complex and powerful face and forehead of Balzac?

Edgar Poe was a little below the average in stature, but solidly built, with small hands and feet. Before his constitution was weakened, he was capable of marvelous feats of strength. One would say that nature, and I believe that this has often been observed, makes life very hard for those from whom she expects great things. Sometimes puny in appearance, they are cut in an athletic mold, they are fit for pleasure or for suffering. While Balzac was attending the rehearsals of the *Ressources de Quinola,* directing and playing all the roles himself, he was correcting proof for his books; he would dine with the actors, and after everyone had gone to bed exhausted, he cheerfully returned to his work. Everyone knows how sober he was and how little sleep he took. As a young man Edgar Poe distinguished himself in every kind of exercise requiring skill and strength; all this had some connection with his talent for calculations and problems. One day he bet that he could dive off the wharf in Richmond, swim up the James River for seven miles, and walk back the same day. And he did it. It was a blazing summer day, and he was none the worse for it. Face, gestures, bearing, demeanor, all showed him, during his earlier years, to be a man of great distinction. He was *marked* by Nature, like those persons who in groups, in restaurants, or on the street, *catch* the eye of the observer and hold it. If ever the word strange, so much abused in contemporary writing, was truly applicable to something, it certainly was with respect to Poe's kind of beauty. His features were not large, but quite regular, his complexion light brown, his face sad and abstracted, and though it revealed neither anger nor insolence, there was something painful about it. His eyes, singularly beautiful, seemed dark grey at first glance, but on closer examination appeared to be tinged with an indefinable light violet tone. As for his forehead, it was superb, not that it recalled the ridiculous proportions that poor artists invent when, in order to flatter genius, they transform it into a hydrocephalus shape, but it seemed that a superabundant inner force was pushing forward the organs of reflection and construction. The parts which phrenologists associate with a sense of the picturesque were nevertheless not lacking, but they seemed disturbed, oppressed, pushed aside by the haughty and greedy tyranny of comparison, of construction and of causality. In the calm pride of this forehead was enthroned the sense of the ideal and of absolute beauty, the esthetic sense par excellence. In spite of all these qualities, his head did not present an agreeable and harmonious whole. Seen from the front, the dominating, inquisitorial expression of the forehead seized and commanded attention, but his profile revealed certain deficiencies; at the front and back the cranial structure was massive, and in the middle it was relatively slight; in short, an enormous physical and intellectual power, and a lack of emotional and spiritual qualities. It is true that the despairing echoes of melancholy which permeate Poe's works have a penetrating accent, but it must be said also that it is a very solitary melancholy, not completely sympathetic to the average man. I cannot help laughing when I think of the lines written shortly after Poe's death by a highly regarded American author, whose name I have forgotten.[15] I am citing from memory, but I can answer for the sense of his remarks: "I have just re-read the works of our lamented Poe. What an admirable poet! What an astonishing storyteller! What a prodigious and superhuman mind! He was certainly the strongest mind in the country! Well, I would gladly give his seventy mystical, analytical and grotesque stories, all so brilliant and full of ideas, for one small wholesome story, a book for the whole family, which he could have written in the marvelously pure style which made him so superior to the rest of us. How much greater Poe would have been!" Ask Edgar Poe to write a book for the whole family! It is true then that human stupidity will always be the same, in all climates, and that critics will always wish to fasten heavy vegetables on rare, exotic plants.

Poe had black hair streaked with a few white lines, a large bristling mustache which he tended to neglect and leave uncombed. He dressed well, but a little carelessly, like a gentleman who has more important things to do. His manners were excellent, very polite and full of assurance. But his conversation deserves particular mention. The first time that I asked an American about it, he laughed a good deal and said: "His talk is *not at all consecutive!*" After some explanation I understood that Poe made long digressions in the world of ideas, like a mathematician making demonstrations for advanced students, and that he tended to monologize. The fact remains that his conversation was essentially instructive. He was not a *glib talker,* and moreover he had a horror of the conventional in his speech as in his writings; but vast learning, the knowledge of several languages, solid studies, ideas gathered in several countries made his talk substantial and informative. In short, for those who measure friendship by spiritual gain, he was a man to know. But it seems that Poe was not at all difficult about his audience. He cared little whether his listeners were able to understand his tenous abstractions, or to admire the glorious conceptions which incessantly illuminated the dark sky of his mind. He would sit down in a tavern, beside some dirty scapegrace, and would gravely explain to him the grand outlines of his terrible book *Eureka* with an implacable composure, as he would have dictated to a secretary, or argued with Kepler, Bacon or Swedenborg. That was a peculiar trait of his character. No man ever freed himself more completely from the rules of society, or bothered himself less about passersby. That explains why on some days he was welcomed in the basement café and refused entrance in the rooms where *respectable people* drink. No society has ever excused such things, least of all English or American society. To begin with, Poe had to be pardoned for his genius; he had launched a terrible attack on mediocrity in the *Southern Literary Messenger;* his criticism had been hard and disciplinary, like that of a superior and solitary man who is interested only in ideas.

There was a moment when he was disgusted with everything human, and when metaphysical speculation alone meant something to him. Dazzling a young and unformed country by his mind, shocking men who considered themselves his equals by his manners, Poe was fated to become a most unhappy writer. Rancors were aroused, solitude settled around him. In Paris, in Germany, he would have found friends who could easily have understood and comforted him; in America, he had to fight for his bread. Thus his drunkenness and nomadic habits are readily explained. He went through life as if through a Sahara desert, and changed his residence like an Arab.

But there are still other reasons: difficult domestic troubles, for instance. We have seen that he was suddenly thrust into the hazards of life at a every early age. Poe was nearly always alone; furthermore, the dreadful strain of mental effort and the bitter difficulties of his work prompted him to find the pleasure of forgetfulness in wine and brandy. He found relief in what causes others fatigue. In a word, literary rancors, the intoxication of the infinite, domestic trials, the affronts of poverty, all these Poe fled in the blackness of drunkenness, as in the blackness of the tomb; for he did not drink like an epicure, but like a barbarian; as soon as alcohol had touched his lips he went to the bar and drank glass after glass until his good Angel was drowned, and all his faculties were destroyed. It is an astonishing fact, but one attested by all who knew him, that neither the purity nor the finish of his style, nor the clearness of his thought, nor his ardor for work and for difficult researches were altered by this terrible habit. The composition of most of his good pieces preceded or followed one of his crises. After the publication of *Eureka* he drank furiously. In New York, on the very morning that *The Whig Review* published *The Raven,* while his name was on every tongue, and when everyone was discussing his poem, he staggered down Broadway, bumping into houses.

Literary drunkenness is one of the most common and deplorable phenomena of modern life; but perhaps there are many attenuating circumstances. In the period of Saint-Amant, de Chapelle and de Colletet, literary persons got drunk also, but joyously, in the company of the noble and the great, who were very lettered, and who were not afraid of *cabarets.* Certain ladies and even young girls were not ashamed to enjoy wine, as is proved by the adventure of a lady whose servant found her with de Chapelle, both of them weeping hot tears after dinner over poor Pindar, who died after being treated by ignorant doctors. The tradition continued in the eighteenth century but changed a little. The school of Rétif was given to drink, but it was already a group of pariahs, a clandestine society. Mercier, when very old, was met one day on the *rue du Coq-Honoré;* Napoleon had recently come to power and Mercier, who was a little drunk, remarked *that he only went on living out of curiosity.* Today, literary drunkenness has taken on a somber and sinister character. There is no longer a special literary class which takes pride in associating with men of letters. Time-absorbing work and the hostilities of different schools prevent their getting together. As for the women, their formless education, their political and literary incompetence keep many writers from seeing in them anything other than household tools or objects of luxury. When dinner is over and the animal has been satisfied, the poet enters the vast solitude of his thought; sometimes he is very fatigued by his labor. What is to become of him then? His mind tells him that he will not lose control, and then he cannot resist the hope of recovering through intoxication the calm or frightening visions which are his old companions. Doubtless the same transformation of manners, which has made literary men a class apart, has caused the immense consumption of tobacco[16] among the new writers.

III

I am going to try to give an idea of the general character which predominates in the works of Edgar Poe. To analyze all of them would be impossible, unless I were to write a whole book, for this strange man, in spite of his disorderly and bedeviled life, produced a great deal. Poe appears in three aspects: critic, poet, and storyteller; moreover, in the storyteller is to be found a philosopher.

When he was invited to be editor of the *Southern Literary Messenger*, it was stipulated that he should receive 2,500 francs a year. In exchange for this very mediocre salary, he was to be responsible for the reading and choice of the selections intended to compose the monthly issues, and for the writing of the editorial section, that is to say the reviewing of new books and the discussion of all current literary events. In addition, he often, very often, contributed a short story or a poem. He continued as editor for almost two years. Thanks to his active management and to the originality of his criticism, the *Southern Literary Messenger* soon attracted all eyes. I have before me a collection of all the issues for these two years: the editorial part is considerable; the articles are very long. Often in the same issue there can be found a review of a novel, of a volume of poetry, of a book on medicine, physics, or history. All are done with the greatest care, and reveal in the author a knowledge of different literatures and a scientific aptitude which bring to mind the French writers of the eighteenth century. It seems that during the preceding years of poverty and hardship Edgar Poe had spent his time profitably and had turned over many ideas in his mind. The *Southern Literary Messenger* contains a remarkable collection of critical evaluations of important English and American authors, and often notes on French literature. Whence came an idea, what was its origin, its purpose, to what school it belonged, what was the author's method, salutary or dangerous, all this was precisely, clearly, and rapidly explained. If Poe attracted a great deal of attention, he also made many enemies. Firm in his convictions, he made indefatigable war upon false reasoning, silly imitations, solecisms, barbarisms, and all the literary offenses perpetrated every day in newspapers and books. In these respects no fault could be found with him, for he practiced what he preached; his style is pure, adequate to his ideas and expresses them exactly. Poe is always correct. It is a very remarkable fact that a man with such a bold and roving imagination should be at the same time so fond of rules and capable of careful analyses and patient research. He might be called an antithesis come to life.

His ability as a critic did much to harm his literary fortune. Many people sought revenge. They spared no pains in hurling reproaches at him as his literary production increased. Everyone is familiar with the long, banal litany: immorality, lack of feeling, lack of conclusions, absurdity, useless literature. Never has French criticism pardoned Balzac for *le Grand homme de province à Paris.*

As a poet, Edgar Poe is a man apart. Almost by himself he represents the romantic movement on the other side of the Atlantic. He is the first American who, properly speaking, has made his style a tool. His poetry, profound and plaintive, is nevertheless carefully wrought, pure, correct, and as brilliant as a crystal jewel. It is obvious that, in spite of astonishing merits, which have made them the idols of weak and sentimental souls, Alfred de Musset and Alphonse de Lamartine would not have been included among Poe's friends, had he lived among us. They lack will power and are not sufficiently masters of themselves. Edgar Poe loved complicated rhythms and, however complicated they were, they contained a profound harmony. There is a short poem of his, entitled *The Bells,* which is a real literary curiosity; it is quite untranslatable. *The Raven* was extremely successful. In the opinion of Longfellow and Emerson, it is a marvel. Its theme is slight, it is a pure work of art. On a stormy, rainy night, a student hears a tapping first at his window and then at his door; he opens, believing it a visitor. It is a poor lost raven which has been attracted by the lamplight. This tamed raven has been taught to speak by another master, and the first word which chances to fall from the beak of the sinister bird penetrates one of the recesses of the student's heart and excites a train of sad, sleeping thoughts: *a woman now dead, a thousand betrayed hopes, a thousand disappointed desires, a broken existence,* a flood of memories which fills the cold and desolate night. The tone is serious and almost supernatural, like the thoughts of a sleepless night; the lines fall one by one, like monotonous tears. In *Dreamland,* he has tried to paint the succession of dreams and fantastic images which besiege the mind when the bodily eye is closed. Other poems, such as *Ulalume* and *Annabel Lee,* are equally famous. But Edgar Poe's poetic output is slight. His poetry, condensed and studied, doubtless cost him much effort, and he needed money too often to devote himself to this pleasurable and unprofitable labor.

As a novelist and storyteller, Edgar Poe is unique in his field, as were Maturin, Balzac, and Hoffmann in theirs. The different stories which he scattered through the reviews have been gathered together in two collections, one, *Tales of the Grotesque and Arabesque,* the other, *Edgar A. Poe's Tales,* edited by Wiley and Putnam. In all they comprise a total of nearly seventy-two pieces. They contain violent buffoonery, the pure grotesque, passionate aspirations toward the infinite, and a great interest in magnetism. The small edition of short stories was as successful in Paris as in America, because it contains very dramatic things, but a most unusual form of the dramatic.

I wish I could characterize the literature of Poe very briefly and very categorically, for it is a quite new literature. What gives it its essential character and distinguishes it among all others is, if I may use these strange words, conjecturism and probabilism. My statement may be verified by a consideration of some specific examples.

The Gold Bug: an analysis of the logical steps to be used in solving a cryptogram, with the help of which a hidden treasure can be found. I cannot help thinking sorrowfully that the unfortunate Poe must have dreamed more than once of ways to discover treasures. How logical and lucid is the explanation of this method which constitutes the curious literary speciality of certain police officers! How delightful is the description of the treasure and what a pleasant feeling of warmth and amazement the reader experiences! For the treasure is found! *It was not a dream,* as is usually the case in all those novels where the author brutually wakens us after exciting our minds with tantalizing hopes; this time it is a *real* treasure, and the decipherer has indeed won it. Here is the exact amount: in money, four hundred and fifty thousand dollars, not a particle of silver, but all in gold and very ancient; the pieces very large and very heavy, the inscriptions illegible; one hundred and ten diamonds, eighteen rubies, three hundred and ten emeralds, twenty-one sapphires and one opal; two hundred massive rings and earrings, about thirty necklaces, eighty-three crucifixes, five censers, an enormous gold punch bowl with vine leaves and bacchants, two sword hilts, one hundred and ninety-seven watches studded with jewels. The contents of the chest is first valued at a million and a half dollars, but the sale of the jewels brings the total to far more than that. The description of this treasure arouses delusions of grandeur and benevolent impulses. In the chest hidden by pirate Kidd there was certainly the means to alleviate many unknown miseries.

A Descent into the Maelstrom: could one not descend into a bottomless whirlpool while studying the laws of gravity in a new way?

Murders in the Rue Morgue: could be helpful to criminal lawyers. A murder has been committed. How? By whom? There are inexplicable and contradictory facts in the case. The police give up. A young man appears who proceeds to review the investigation out of esthetic interest.

By extreme concentration of thought and by the successive analysis of all the phenomena of his own mental processes, he has succeeded in discovering the law of the genesis of ideas. Between one word and another, between two ideas completely foreign to each other on the surface, he is able to reestablish the whole intermediary series, and to fill in astonishingly the lacuna of unexpressed and almost unconscious ideas. He carefully studies all the possible and all the probable interrelations of the facts. He proceeds from induction to induction and manages to prove conclusively that it was an ape that committed the crime.

Mesmeric Revelation: the author's point of departure has obviously been this: would it not be possible to discover the law which governs distant worlds with the help of the unknown force called magnetism? The beginning is full of grandeur and solemnity. The doctor has mesmerized his patient only to comfort him. "How do you think your present illness will result?" —"I must die." —"Does the idea of death afflict you?" —"No." The patient complains that he is not being questioned properly. "What then shall I ask?" says the doctor. "You must begin at the beginning." —"But where is the beginning?" —(In a very low voice.) —"Is not God spirit?" —"No." —"Is God, then, material?" —"No." There follows a very comprehensive theory of matter, of the gradations of matter and of the hierarchy of beings. I published this story in one of the issues of *Liberté de penser* in 1848.[17]

Elsewhere we have the story of a soul which once lived on a planet that had disappeared.[18] The point of departure is: can one, by means of induction and analysis, guess what would be the physical and moral phenomena among the inhabitants of a world which was being approached by a destructive comet?

At other times we find pure fantasy, modeled on nature and realistically presented, in the manner of Hoffmann: *The Man of the Crowd* constantly plunges into the midst of crowds; he swims with delight in the human ocean. When twilight comes filled with trembling lights and shadows, he flees from the quiet of peaceful places and eagerly goes in search of those that swarm with human activity. As the circle of light and life grows smaller, he seeks the center with a feeling of anxiety; like men caught in a flood he clings desperately to the final vestiges of public excitement. And that is all. Is he a criminal who is afraid of solitude? Is he a silly fool who cannot endure his own company?

What Parisian author who is at all well read is not acquainted with *The Black Cat?* Here we find virtues of a different order. In what a sweet and innocent manner this terrible poem of crime begins! "My wife and I were drawn together by many mutual tastes, and by a fondness for animals which had been encouraged by our parents. As a result, our house was like a menagerie; we had every kind of pet imaginable." Things go badly for them. Instead of acting, the man shuts himself up in the black dreams of the tavern. The beautiful black cat, the lovable Pluto, who once was so attentive on his master's return, shows him less attention and affection; he even seems to flee him and to scent the dangers of brandy and gin. The man is offended. His melancholy, his taciturn and solitary mood increase as the habit of drink grows. How well Poe has described the somber life of the tavern, the silent hours of gloomy drunkenness.[19] And yet it is rapid and brief. The mute reproach of the animal exasperates him more and more. One evening for some strange reason he seizes the animal, takes his knife, and cuts out one of its eyes. Thenceforth the one-eyed, bloody animal will flee from him and as a result the man's hate will continue to grow. Finally he strangles the cat by hanging. This passage deserves to be cited:

> In the meantime the cat slowly recovered. The socket of the lost eye presented, it is true, a frightful appearance, but he no longer appeared to suffer any pain. He went about the house as usual, but, as might be expected, fled in extreme terror at my approach. I had so much of my old heart left, as to be at first grieved by this evident dislike on the part of a creature which had once so loved me. But this feeling soon gave place to irritation. And then came, as if to my final and irrevocable overthrow, the spirit of PERVERSENESS. Of this spirit philosophy takes no account. Yet I am not more sure that my soul lives, than I am that perverseness is one of the primitive impulses of the human heart—one of the in-

> divisible primary faculties, or sentiments, which give direction to the character of Man. Who has not, a hundred times, found himself committing a vile or a stupid action, for no other reason than because he knows he should *not?* Have we not a perpetual inclination, in the teeth of our best judgment, to violate that which is *Law,* merely because we understand it to be such? This spirit of perverseness, I say, came to my final overthrow. It was this unfathomable longing of the soul *to vex itself*—to offer violence to its own nature—to do wrong for the wrong's sake only —that urged me to continue and finally to consummate the injury I had inflicted upon the unoffending brute. One morning, in cold blood, I slipped a noose about its neck and hung it to the limb of a tree;—hung it with the tears streaming from my eyes, and with the bitterest remorse at my heart;—hung it *because* I knew that it had loved me, and *because* I felt it had given me no reason of offense;—hung it *because* I knew that in so doing I was committing a sin—a deadly sin that would so jeopardize my immortal soul as to place it—if such a thing were possible—even beyond the reach of the infinite mercy of the Most Merciful and Most Terrible God.

A fire completes the ruin of the couple and forces them to take refuge in a poor section of the city. The man continues to drink. His disease makes frightful progress, "*for what disease is like Alcohol?*" One evening he notices on one of the hogsheads of the tavern a very beautiful black cat exactly resembling Pluto. The animal allows itself to be approached and returns his caresses. He takes it home to console his wife. The next day it is discovered that the cat is blind in one eye, and in the same eye. This time it is the affectionate nature of the cat that slowly exasperates him; its wearisome attentions seem to him to be a kind of Nemesis, irony, and accusation embodied in a mysterious animal. It is evident that the wretched man has become slightly mad. One evening as he is going down into the cellar with his wife on some household errand, the faithful cat accompanying them brushes against him and almost trips him. Furious, the man tries to attack it; the wife intervenes; he kills her on the spot with the blow of an axe. His first thought is how to conceal the body. He decides to put it in a wall which he then plasters up with mortar that has been cleverly mixed with dirt. The cat has disappeared. "He understood my anger and thought it wise to run away." Our man sleeps the sleep of the just; and in the morning at sunrise he feels immense joy and relief not to have his awakening tormented by the odious caresses of the animal. However, the police make several investigations of the premises and, thoroughly satisfied, are about to depart when suddenly: "You forget the cellar, Gentlemen," he said. They visit the cellar and as they go up the stairs without having found any compromising evidence, "seized with a diabolical idea and with the frenzy of an incredible bravado, I cried: a fine wall! fine construction, indeed! they don't make walls like these any more! And saying this, I struck the wall with my cane at the very spot where the victim was hidden."[20] A cry, low, distant, and plaintive, is heard; the man faints; the police stop, tear down the wall, the corpse falls forward and a terrifying cat, half fur, half plaster, springs out with its solitary, bloody, and wild eye.

Not only probabilities and possibilities strongly aroused Poe's ardent curiosity, but also maladies of the mind. *Berenice* is an admirable example of this genre; however improbable and exaggerated my dry analysis may make it appear, I can assure the reader that nothing is more logical and possible than this terrible story. Egaeus and Berenice are cousins; Egaeus, pale and devoted to theosophy, frail and overtaxing his intellectual powers to gain an understanding of abstruse things; Berenice, carefree and lighthearted, always in the open air, in the woods and the garden, admirably beautiful with a luminous and physical beauty. Berenice is attacked by a mysterious and horrible malady mentioned somewhere under the rather strange name of *distortion of personality*. It might be said that it is a kind of hysteria. She also suffers epileptic attacks, frequently followed by a trance closely resembling death from which her recovery is usually startlingly abrupt. Her wonderful beauty fades away, so to speak, in dissolution. As for Egaeus, his illness, for so, he says, it was called in everyday language, is even more strange. It consists in a highly exaggerated development of the meditative powers, a morbid stimulation of the *attentive* faculties. "To muse for long unwearied hours, with my attention riveted to some frivolous device on the margin or in the typography of a book; to become absorbed, for the better part of a summer's day, in a quaint shadow falling aslant upon the tapestry or upon the floor; to lose myself, for an entire night, in watching the steady flame of a lamp, or the embers of a fire, to dream away whole days over the perfume of a flower; to repeat, monotonously, some common word, until the sound, by dint of frequent repetition, ceased to convey any idea whatever to the mind; to lose all sense of motion or physical existence, by means of absolute bodily quiescence long and obstinately persevered in: such were a few of the most common and least pernicious vagaries induced by a condition of the mental faculties, not, indeed, altogether unparalleled, but certainly bidding defiance to any thing like analysis or explanation." And he takes good care to point out that his is not the exaggerated daydreaming common to all men; for the dreamer takes an interesting object as a point of departure, he proceeds from deduction to deduction, and after a long day spent in musing, the first cause has completely vanished, the *incitamentum* has disappeared. In the case of Egaeus, the contrary is true. The object is invaribly trivial; but through the medium of a distempered vision, it assumes a refracted importance. Few deductions, no pleasant meditations; and finally, the first cause, very far from being out of sight, has attained a preternatural interest; it has taken on an abnormal importance which is the distinctive characteristic of this illness.

Egaeus is about to marry his cousin. At the time of her incomparable beauty, he had never spoken a single word of love to her; but he feels a great fondness and a great pity for her. Besides, does she not offer the immense attraction of a problem? And, as he admits, *in the strange anomaly of his existence, his emotions never came from his heart, and his passions always came from his mind.*[21] One evening, in the library, Berenice stands before him. Either because of his troubled mind or because of the influence of the twilight, he imagines her to be taller than usual. For a long time he looks speechless at that emaciated phantom which, with the pathetic coquetry of a once beautiful woman, essays a smile, a smile which seems to say: "I am very changed, am I not?" And then she discloses all her teeth between her poor twisted lips. "Would to God that I had never beheld them, or that, having done so, I had died!"

And now the teeth have become a fixed obsession in the man's mind. For two days and a night he remains nailed to the same spot with the teeth seeming to encompass him. The teeth are daguerreotyped in his brain, long, narrow, like the teeth of a dead horse; not a spot, not an indenture, not a point escaped his mind. He shivers with horror when he realizes that he has attributed to them a power of emotion and a capability of moral expression, even when unassisted by the lips. "Of Mademoiselle Sallé it has been well said *that all her steps were feelings,* and of Berenice I more seriously believed *that all her teeth were ideas.*"[22]

Toward the end of the second day Berenice died. Egaeus does not dare refuse to enter the death chamber to say a last farewell to the remains of his cousin. The coffin has been placed on the bed. The heavy curtains of the bed which he raises fall back upon his shoulders and confine him in the closest communion with the deceased. Strange trick of fate, a band which held together her jaws had become untied. Long and white, the teeth shine implacably. He tears himself violently away from the bed and leaves terrified.

Thereafter darkness clouds his mind, and the story becomes blurred and confused. He finds himself sitting in the library at a table with a lamp, a book open before him, and his eyes seem to start from his head when they fall upon this sentence: "*Dicebant mihi sodales si sepulchrum amicae visitarem, curas meas aliquantulum fore levatas.*" By his side, an ebony box. Why that ebony box? Does it not belong to the family doctor? A servant enters, pale and troubled: he speaks in a low and indistinct voice. In broken sentences he tells of a violated grave, of loud cries that had been heard, of a corpse still warm and breathing that had been found all bloody and mutilated near the edge of the pit. He points to the clothes of Egaeus; they are muddy and covered with blood. He takes him by the hand; it bears strange imprints, lacerations made by human nails. He calls his attention to a tool which rests against the wall. It is a spade. With a horrible cry Egaeus seizes the box; but in his weakness and excitement he drops it, and the box, in falling, scatters instruments of dental surgery over the floor, mingling the frightful sound of metal with the accursed objects of his hallucination. The wretched man, in a moment of mental aberration, had gone to the grave of his cousin, who had been buried after an attack resembling death, and had snatched from her jaws the objects of his obsession.

Usually Edgar Poe suppresses minor details, or at least gives them only a very insignificant importance. As a result of this cruel restraint, the basic idea is more clearly perceived and the theme stands out sharply against this bare background. As for his method of narration, it is simple. He overuses *I* with a cynical monotony. It could be said that he is so sure of holding the reader's interest that he worries very little about varying his means. His short stories are almost always the personal accounts or manuscripts of the protagonist. As for his intense preoccupation with the horrible, I have noticed among a number of men that it was often the result of an immense unused vital energy, or sometimes of a stubborn chastity, or of a deeply repressed sensibility.

The unnatural pleasure that a man may feel on seeing his own blood flow, brusque and useless movements, loud cries uttered almost involuntarily are analogous phenomena. Pain relieves pain, action rests one from repose.

Another characteristic of his writing is that it is completely anti-feminine. Let me explain myself. Women write and write, with an exuberant rapidity; their hearts speak and chatter in reams. Usually they know nothing of art, or measure, or logic; their style trails and flows like their garments. A very great and a very justly famous writer, George Sand[23] herself, has not altogether escaped this law of temperament in spite of her superiority; she dashes off her masterpieces as if she were writing letters. Has it not been said that she writes her books on stationery?

In the books of Edgar Poe the style is compact and *concatenated;* the prejudice or the inertia of the reader cannot penetrate the meshes of this network woven by logic. All his ideas, like obedient arrows, fly to the same target.

I have perused a long series of short stories without finding one love story. So fascinating is this man that I only realized it afterwards. Without meaning to praise unreservedly the ascetic system of an ambitious soul, I think that a severe literature in our country would constitute a useful protest against the encroaching *conceit* of women, which has been more and more encouraged by the disgusting idolatry of men; and I strongly sympathize with Voltaire who, in his preface to *la Mort de César,* a tragedy without women, thought it well to call attention to his noteworthy *tour de force* under cover of feigned excuses for his impertinence.

In Edgar Poe there is no tiresome snivelling; but everywhere and at all times an indefatigable enthusiasm in seeking the ideal. He has a passion for science like Balzac, who died grieved perhaps at not being a pure scientist. He has written a work called *The Conchologist's First Book* which I have forgotten to mention. He has, like conquerors and philosophers, a compelling yearning for unity; he combines the spiritual with the physical. It could be said that he seeks to apply to literature the processes of philosophy, and to philosophy the methods of algebra. In this constant ascension toward the infinite, one becomes somewhat breathless. The air in this literature is as rarefied as that of a laboratory. In it can be observed continually the glorification of the will applying itself to induction and to analysis. It seems that Poe wants to usurp the role of the prophets and to claim for himself a monopoly on rational explanation. Thus the landscapes which sometimes serve as a background for his febrile compositions are pale as phantoms. Poe, who scarcely seemed to share the passions of other men, sketches trees and clouds which are like the trees and clouds of a dream, or rather which resemble his strange characters and which are agitated like them by a supernatural and convulsive shudder.

Once, however, he set himself the task of writing a purely human book. *The Narrative of Arthur Gordon Pym,*[24] which has not been very successful, is a story of sailors who, after serious damage to their ship, have been becalmed in the South Seas. The genius of the author revels in these terrible scenes and in the amazing descriptions of islands and tribes which are not indicated on any map. The execution of this book is extremely simple and detailed. Moreover, it is done in the form of a log book. The ship has become unmanageable; the supplies of food and drinking water are exhausted; the sailors are reduced to cannibalism. However, a brig is sighted.

> No person was seen upon her decks until she arrived within about a quarter of a mile of us. We then saw three seamen, whom by their dress we took to be Hollanders. Two of these were lying on some old sails near the forecastle, and the third, who appeared to be looking at us with great curiosity, was leaning over the starboard bow near the bowsprit. This last was a stout and tall man, with a very dark skin. He seemed by his manner to be encouraging us to have patience, nodding to us in a cheerful although rather odd way, and smiling constantly, so as to display a set of the most brilliantly white teeth. As his vessel drew nearer, we saw a red flannel cap which he had on fall from his head into the water; but of this he took little or no notice, continuing his odd smiles and gesticulations. I relate these things and circumstances minutely, and I relate them, it must be understood, precisely as they *appeared* to us.
>
> The brig came on slowly, and now more steadily than before, and—I cannot speak calmly of this event—our hearts leaped up wildly within us, and we poured out our whole souls in shouts and thanksgiving to God for the complete, unexpected, and glorious deliverance that was so palpably at hand. Of a sudden, and all at once, there came wafted over the ocean from the strange vessel (which was now close upon us) a smell, a stench, such as the whole world has no name for—no conception of—hellish—utterly suffocating—insufferable, inconceivable. I gasped for breath, and turning to my companions, perceived that they were paler than marble. But we

had now no time left for question or surmise—the brig was within fifty feet of us, and it seemed to be her intention to run under our counter, that we might board her without putting out a boat. We rushed aft, when, suddenly, a wide yaw threw her off full five or six points from the course she had been running, and, as she passed under our stern at the distance of about twenty feet, we had a full view of her decks. Shall I ever forget the triple horror of that spectacle? Twenty-five or thirty human bodies, among whom were several females, lay scattered about between the counter and the galley in the last and most loathsome state of putrefaction. We plainly saw that not a soul lived in that fated vessel! Yet we could not help shouting to the dead for help! Yes, long and loudly did we beg, in the agony of the moment, that those silent and disgusting images would stay for us, would not abandon us to become like them, would receive us among their goodly company! We were raving with horror and despair—thoroughly mad through the anguish of our grievous disappointment.

As our first loud yell of terror broke forth, it was replied to by something, from near the bowsprit of the stranger, so closely resembling the scream of a human voice that the nicest ear might have been startled and deceived. At this instant another sudden yaw brought the region of the forecastle for a moment into view, and we beheld at once the origin of the sound. We saw the tall stout figure still leaning on the bulwark, and still nodding his head to and fro, but his face was now turned from us so that we could not behold it. His arms were extended over the rail, and the palms of his hands fell outward. His knees were lodged upon a stout rope, tightly stretched, and reaching from the heel of the bowsprit to a cathead. On his back, from which a portion of the shirt had been torn, leaving it bare, there sat a huge sea-gull, busily gorging itself with the horrible flesh, its bill and talons deeply buried, and its white plumage spattered all over with blood. As the brig moved farther round so as to bring us close in view, the bird, with much apparent difficulty, drew out its crimsoned head, and, after eyeing us for a moment as if stupefied, arose lazily from the body upon which it had been feasting, and, flying directly above our deck, hovered there a while with a portion of clotted and liver-like substance in its beak. The horrid morsel dropped at length with a sullen splash immediately at the feet of Parker. May God forgive me, but now, for the first time, there flashed through my mind a thought, a thought which I will not mention, and I felt myself making a step toward the ensanguined spot. I looked upward, and the eyes of Augustus met my own with a degree of intense and eager meaning which immediately brought me to my senses. I sprang forward, quickly, and, with a deep shudder, threw the frightful thing into the sea.

The body from which it had been taken, resting as it did upon the rope, had been easily swayed to and fro by the exertions of the carnivorous bird, and it was this motion which had at first impressed us with the belief of its being alive. As the gull relieved it of its weight, it swung round and fell partially over, so that the face was fully discovered. Never, surely, was any object so terribly full of awe! The eyes were gone, and the whole flesh around the mouth, leaving the teeth utterly naked. This, then, was the smile which had cheered us on to hope! this the—but I forebear. The brig, as I have already told, passed under our stern, and made its way slowly but steadily to leeward. With her and with her terrible crew went all our gay visions of deliverance and joy.

Eureka was doubtless Poe's most cherished and long dreamed of book.[25] I cannot give a very exact account of it here. It is a book which requires a special article. Whoever has read *Mesmeric Revelation* knows the metaphysical tendencies of our author. *Eureka* purports to develop the procedure and to demonstrate the law according to which the universe has assumed its present visible form and found its present organization, and also how this same law, which was the origin of its creation, will be the means of its destruction and of the final dissolution of the world. It can be easily understood why I do not care to undertake lightly the discussion of so ambitious a project. I should be afraid of going astray and of slandering an author for whom I have the most profound respect. Edgar Poe has already been accused of being a pantheist, and although I am forced to admit that appearances encourage this belief, I can affirm that, like many other great men fond of logic, he is sometimes very inconsistent, which is to his credit; thus his pantheism runs counter to his ideas on the hierarchy of beings and to many passages which obviously affirm the permanence of personalities.

Edgar Poe was very proud of this book which did not enjoy, and very naturally so, the success of his short stories. It must be read carefully and his strange ideas must be verified by the juxtaposition of analogous and contrary systems.

IV

I had a friend who was also a metaphysician in his way, enthusiastic and positive, with the air of a Saint-Just.[26] He often used to tell me, while citing some example among his contemporaries and looking at me suspicously: "Every mystic has a hidden vice." And I concluded his thought within myself: then it must be destroyed. But I laughed because I did not understand him. One day as I was talking to a well known and very prosperous bookdealer, who specializes in serving the interests of all the mystics and of the obscure disciples of the occult sciences, and as I was asking him about his clients, he said to me: "Remember that every mystic has a hidden vice, often one that is very worldly; drunkenness in one case, gluttony in another, and lechery in still another; one will be very miserly, another very cruel, etc."

Heavens! I said to myself, what is this fatal law which enchains us, dominates us, and wreaks vengeance for the violation of its unbearable despotism through the degredation and the weakening of our moral being? Visionaries have been the greatest of men. Why must they be punished for their greatness? Was not their ambition most noble? Will man eternally be so limited that one of his faculties can develop only at the expense of the others? If to wish to know truth at any price is a great crime, or can lead to great faults, if foolishness and thoughtlessness are virtues and a guarantee of stability, I think that we ought to be very indulgent toward these guilty men of renown, for this same vice can be ascribed to all of us who are children of the eighteenth and nineteenth centuries.

I say without shame, because I feel that it springs from a profound sense of pity and affection, that I prefer Edgar Poe, drunk, poor, persecuted, and a pariah, to a calm and virtuous Goethe or Walter Scott. I should willingly say of him and of a special class of men what the catechism says of our Lord: "He has suffered much for us."

One could write on his tomb: "All you who have ardently sought to discover the laws of your being, who have aspired to the infinite, and whose repressed emotions have had to seek a frightful relief in wine and debauchery, pray for him. Now his purified corporeal being soars amid beings whose existence he glimpsed; pray for him who sees and who knows, he will intercede for you."[27]

Edgar Poe

Sa Vie et Ses Oeuvres: 1856

. . . Quelque maître malheureux à qui l'inexorable Fatalité a donné une chasse acharnée, toujours plus acharnée, jusqu'à ce que ses chants n'aient plus qu'un unique refrain, jusqu'à ce que les chants funèbres de son Espérance aient adopté ce mélancolique refrain: Jamais! Jamais plus!

Edgar Poe. *Le Corbeau*

Sur son trône d'airain le Destin qui s'en raille
Imbibe leur éponge avec du fiel amer,
Et la Nécessité les tord dans sa tenaille.

Théophile Gautier. *Ténèbres*

I

Dans ces derniers temps, un malheureux fut amené devant nos tribunaux, dont le front était illustré d'un rare et singulier tatouage: PAS DE CHANCE! *Il portait ainsi au-dessus de ses yeux l'étiquette de sa vie, comme un livre son titre, et l'interrogatoire prouva que ce biz-*

. . . Caught from some unhappy master whom unmerciful Disaster
Followed fast and followed faster till his songs one burden bore—
Till the dirges of his hope that melancholy burden bore of 'Never—nevermore.'

Edgar Poe. *The Raven*

On his throne of brass mocking Destiny soaks their sponge in bitter gall, and Necessity twists them in its vise.

Théophile Gautier. *Ténèbres*

I

Recently there appeared in court an unfortunate man whose forehead was marked by a rare and strange tattoo: *No luck!* He bore thus above his eyes the inscription of his life, like the title of a book, and cross-examination showed that this bizarre label was cruelly true. In literary history there are similar destinies, real damnations,—men who bear the words *bad luck* written in mysterious characters in the sinuous creases of their foreheads. The blind Angel of expiation has seized upon them and whips them with all his might for the edification of others. In vain their lives show talents, virtues, graces; for them Society has a special curse, and accuses them of the weaknesses that its persecution has produced.—What did not Hoffmann do to disarm destiny and what did not Balzac undertake to charm fortune?—Is there then a diabolical Providence which prepares misfortune in the cradle,—which *deliberately* thrusts spiritual and angelic natures into hostile surroundings, like martyrs into the circus? Are there then *consecrated* souls, destined for the altar, condemned to march to death and glory through their own ruins? Will the nightmare of Darkness besiege these exceptional souls eternally?—In vain they struggle, in vain they adapt themselves to the calculations and tricks of the world; they may be perfect in prudence, they may stop up every opening, they may stuff the windows against the missiles of chance; but the Devil will come in through a keyhole; perfection will be the flaw in their armor, and superlative excellence the germ of their damnation.

The eagle from on high will drop a tortoise on their bare heads in order to shatter [*their hopes*], *for they are inevitably destined to perish.*[1]

Their destiny is written in their whole being, it shines with a sinister brilliance in their eyes and in their gestures, it circulates in their arteries with each drop of blood.

A famous contemporary writer has written a book[2] to show that the poet cannot find a good place either in a democratic society or in an aristocratic one, no more in a republic than in an absolute or constitutional monarchy. Who has been able to give him a conclusive answer? Today I have a new story to support his thesis, I am adding a new saint to the martyrology; I have to write the history of an illustrious failure, too rich in poetry and passion, who came, after so many others in this base world, to serve the harsh apprenticeship of genius among inferior spirits.

What a grievous tragedy was the life of Edgar Poe! What a horrible ending was his death, the horror of which was increased by vulgar circumstances!—All the documents that I have read lead to the conviction that for Poe the United States was nothing more than a vast prison which he traversed with the feverish agitation of a being made to breathe a sweeter air,—nothing more than a great gas-lighted nightmare,—and that his inner, spiritual life, as a poet or even as a drunkard, was nothing but a perpetual effort to escape the influence of this unfriendly atmosphere. In democratic societies public opinion is a pitiless dictator; do not ask of it any charity, any indulgence, any elasticity whatever in the application of its laws to the manifold and complex cases of moral life. It could be said that from the impious love of liberty a new tyranny has been born, the tyranny of animals, or zoöcracy, which in its ferocious insensibility resembles the Juggernaut.—A biographer[3] will tell us in all seriousness,—the good man means well,—that if Poe had been willing to normalize his genius and to apply his creative faculties in a way appropriate to the American soil, he could have become a money-making author; another,—[4] this one a naïve cynic,—that however beautiful the genius of Poe may have been, it would have been better for him to have possessed only talent, since talent always pays off more readily than genius. Another,[5] who was a newspaper and magazine editor, a friend of the poet, admits that it was difficult to employ him and that it was necessary to pay him less than others, because he wrote in a style too much above the ordinary level. *What a commercial smell!* as Joseph de Maistre would say.

Some have gone even further, and joining the dullest incomprehension of his genius to the ferocity of bourgeois hypocrisy, have outdone themselves in insults;

and after his sudden death, they harshly lectured his corpse,—especially Mr. Rufus Griswold who, to recall the bitter remark of Mr. George Graham, then committed an imperishable infamy. Poe, perhaps feeling a sinister premonition of his sudden end, had asked Griswold and Willis to put his works in order, to write his biography and keep alive his memory. That pedagogical vampire defamed his friend at great length in a flat and hateful article published as the introduction of the posthumous edition of Poe's works. Is there then no ordinance in America which forbids dogs to enter cemeteries? On the other hand, Willis has shown that kindness and decency always accompany true intelligence, and that charity towards our fellow men, which is a moral duty, is also one of the commandments of taste.

Talk to an American about Poe and he will perhaps admit his genius; perhaps he will even show himself proud of it. But, with a superior, sardonic tone, which smacks of practicality, he will speak to you of the irregular life of the poet, of his alcoholic breath that could have been set on fire with a candle, of his vagabond habits; he will tell you that Poe was an erratic and eccentric person, a stray planet, that he moved constantly from Baltimore to New York, from New York to Philadelphia, from Philadelphia to Boston, from Boston to Baltimore, from Baltimore to Richmond. And if, moved by these preludes of a disheartening story, you suggest that he was perhaps not the only guilty party, and that it must be difficult to think and write readily in a country which has millions of rulers, a country without a great capital and without an aristocracy,—

then you will see his eyes open and flash lightning, the slaver of outraged patriotism rising to his lips, and you will hear America, through his mouth, hurl insults at Europe, its old mother, and at the philisophy of former times.

I repeat my conviction that Edgar Poe and his country were not on the same level. The United States is a young and gigantic country, naturally jealous of the old continent. Proud of its material development, abnormal and almost monstrous, this newcomer in history has a naïve faith in the omnipotence of industry; it is convinced, like some unfortunate persons among us, that it will succeed in devouring the Devil. Time and money have such a great value there! Material activity, disproportionately emphasized to the point of being a national mania, leaves little room in their minds for things which are not of this world. Poe, who was of good stock and who moreover maintained that the great misfortune of his country was the lack of an aristocracy of birth, since, as he said, among a people without an aristocracy the cult of the Beautiful could only become corrupt, diminish and disappear,—who charged his fellow citizens, in their costly and pretentious luxury, with all the symptons of bad taste characteristic of upstarts,—who considered Progress, the great modern idea, as the fatuous dream of simpletons, and who called the alleged *improvements* in houses eyesores and rectangular abominations,—Poe was an exceptionally solitary mind. He believed only in the immutable, the eternal, the self-same, and he possessed—cruel privilege in a society enamored of itself,—that great Machiavellian good sense which moves in front of a wise man, like a pillar of fire, across the desert of history.—What would he have thought, what would he have written, unhappy man, if he had heard a sentimental theologian[6] abolish Hell through love for the human race, a philosopher of figures propose a system of insurance (a penny per person) to stop war,—and the abolition of capital punishment and spelling, those two related follies!—and how many other sick people who write, *with their ear to the wind*, gyrating fantasies as flatulent as the air that inspires them?—If you add to this impeccable vision of the true, which can be a real weakness in certain circumstances, an exquisite sensitiveness that was distressed by any false note, delicacy of taste that was revolted by anything except exact proportions, an insatiable love of the Beautiful which had become a morbid passion, you will not be surprised that for such a man life should have become hell, and that he should have come to a bad end. You will be astonished that he was able to endure such a long time.

II

Poe's family was one of the most respectable in Baltimore. His maternal grandfather had served as quartermaster-general in the Revolutionary War and had won the esteem and friendship of Lafayette. The latter, during his last visit to the United States wished to call upon the widow of the general and to express his gratitude for the services which her husband had rendered. His great-grandfather had married the daughter of the English admiral McBride, who was connected with the most aristocratic families in England. David Poe, the father of Edgar and the son of the general, fell violently in love with an English actress, Elisabeth Arnold, who was famous for her beauty; they eloped. In order to join his destiny more closely to hers, he became an actor and appeared with his wife in various theaters in the principal cities of the United States. They both died at Richmond, almost at the same time, leaving three young children in the utmost destitution. One of them was Edgar.

Edgar Poe was born in Baltimore in 1813.—I give this date, which is in accordance with his own statement, in contradiction of Griswold who puts his birth in 1811.—If ever the spirit of romance, to use one of his own expressions, presided over a birth,—sinister and stormy spirit!—certainly it presided over his. Poe was truly a child of passion and adventure. A rich merchant of the town, Mr. Allan, took a fancy to the pretty orphaned child whom nature had endowed with a charming manner and, since he had no children, he adopted him.[7] Henceforth his name was Edgar Allan Poe. Thus he was brought up in easy circumstances and with the legitimate hope of one of those fortunes that give character a superb certitude. His foster parents took him on a trip to England, Scotland and Ireland, and, before returning home, they left him with Dr. Bransby, who was the director of an important school at Stoke Newington, near London.—Poe himself, in *William Wilson*, has described that strange place, built in the old Elizabethan style, as well as the impressions of his school days.

He returned to Richmond in 1822 and continued his studies in America under the best available masters.

At the University of Virginia, which he entered in 1825, he distinguished himself not only by a nearly miraculous intelligence, but also by an almost sinister abundance of passions,—a truly American form of precocity, —which finally led to his expulsion. It is worth noting in passing that already at Charlottesville, Poe had shown a most remarkable aptitude for physical science and mathematics. Later he will make frequent use of it in his strange stories, and will draw from it very unexpected technical resources. But I have reason to believe that he did not attach the greatest importance to compositions of this type, and that,—perhaps even because of his precocious aptitude,—he was inclined to consider them facile tricks compared to works of pure imagination. — Some unfortunate gambling debts brought about a momentary quarrel between him and his foster father, and Edgar,—a most curious fact, and one which proves, whatever one may say, that there was a rather considerable amount of chivalry in his impressionable mind,—conceived the idea of taking part in the Greek Revolution and of going away to fight the Turks. He left for Greece.—What became of him in the Orient, what did he do there,—did he study the classic shores of the Mediterranean,—why do we find him in Saint Petersburg, without a passport,—compromised, and in what sort of affair,—obliged to call upon the American ambassador, Henry Middleton, in order to escape a Russian sentence and return home?—we do not know; there is a lacuna that only he could fill in. The life of Edgar Poe, his youth, his adventures in Russia and his correspondence have been promised by American magazines for a long time and have never appeared.

Once more in America, in 1829, he expressed the desire to enter West Point; he was admitted, and there as elsewhere showed the signs of an admirably well endowed but undisciplinable intelligence, and after a few months he was dropped.—In this adoptive family there was taking place at the same time an event which was to have the most serious effects on his whole life. Mrs. Allan, for whom he seems to have felt a truly filial affection, died, and Mr. Allan married a very young woman. A domestic quarrel took place,—a vague and bizarre story which I cannot tell, because it has not been clearly explained by any biographer. Thus there is no reason to be surprised that he should have broken completely with Mr. Allan, and that the latter, who had children by his second marriage, should have cut him off from his inheritance.

Shortly after leaving Richmond, Poe published a small volume of poems; it was indeed a remarkable beginning. Whoever has a feeling for English poetry will find there already the unearthly accent, the calm melancholy, the delightful solemnity, the precocious experience,—I believe I was about to say *innate experience,*[8]—which characterizes the great poets.

For a time poverty forced him to become a soldier, and presumably he used the wearisome garrison hours to prepare the material of his future compositions,—strange compositions which seem to have been created in order to show us that strangeness is one of the integral parts of the beautiful. Having returned to literary life, the only element in which certain classless beings can breathe, Poe was wasting away in utter destitution, when a happy chance put him on his feet again. The owner of a review had just offered two prizes, one for the best short story, the other for the best poem. An exceptionally beautiful handwriting attracted the eyes of Mr. Kennedy, who was chairman of the committee, and stimulated him to read the manuscripts himself. It turned out that Poe had won both prizes; but he was given only one.[9] The chairman of the jury was curious to meet the unknown writer. The editor of the magazine introduced him to a strikingly handsome young man, in rags, his coat buttoned up to his chin, who had the air of a gentleman as proud as he was hungry. Kennedy acted well. He introduced Poe to Mr. Thomas White, who was establishing the *Southern Literary Messenger* at Richmond. Mr. White was a bold man, but without any literary talent; he needed an assistant. Quite young then, —at the age of twenty-two,—Poe found himself the director of a magazine whose destiny depended entirely on him. He created the prosperity which it enjoyed. Since then the *Southern Literary Messenger* has recognized that it was to this wretched eccentric, to this incorrigible drunkard that it owed its circulation and its fruitful notoriety. It was in this magazine that there first appeared *The Unparalleled Adventure of One Hans Pfaall* and several other stories which our readers will see. For nearly two years, Edgar Poe, with a marvelous ardor, astonished his public by a series of compositions of a new type and by critical articles whose liveliness, clearness and reasoned severity were well calculated to attract attention. These articles had to do with books of all sorts, and the excellent education which the young man had had served him well. It is well to remember that this considerable task was done for five hundred dollars, that is to say 2,700 francs a year. *Immediately,* —writes Griswold, by which he means to say: Poe thought himself sufficiently well off, the imbecile!—he married a beautiful and charming young girl, amiable and heroic, but *without a cent,*—adds this same Griswold, with a tone of contempt. She was a Miss Virginia Clemm, his cousin.

In spite of the services which he had performed for the magazine, Mr. White quarreled with Poe after about two years. The poet's attacks of hypochondria and drunkenness were apparently the cause of the separation,—characteristic occurrences which darkened his spiritual sky, like those ominous clouds which suddenly give the most romantic landscape a seemingly irreparable air of melancholy.—From that time on, we shall see the ill-fated man move his tent, like a nomad of the desert, and carry his portable household gods to the principal cities of the Union. Everywhere he will edit reviews or contribute to them in a brilliant manner. With a dazzling rapidity he will pour out critical and philosophical articles, and stories full of magic which were later published under the title: *Tales of the Grotesque and the Arabesque,*—a carefully chosen title, for grotesque and arabesque ornaments reject the human figure, and it will be seen that in many respects Poe's writing is outside or above the human. Scandalous and offensive notices appearing in newspapers inform us that Poe and his wife were dangerously ill at Fordham and in absolute poverty. Soon after the death of Mrs. Poe, the poet experienced the first attacks of *delirium tremens.* Suddenly a new assault appeared in a paper, —this one more than cruel,—which assailed his scorn and his disgust for the world, and put him on trial, a real public inquisition, such as he always had to face,—one of the most sterile and fatiguing struggles that I know.

Doubtless he was making money, and his literary work almost provided him with a living. But I have proof that he had to overcome humiliating difficulties constantly. Like so many other writers, he dreamed of a journal of his own, he wanted to be *at home,* and he had certainly suffered enough to wish ardently for that definite shelter for his thought. In order to obtain enough money for that purpose, he resorted to giving lectures. You know what they are like,—a kind of speculation, the university put at the disposal of literary persons, the author publishing his lecture only after having drawn from it all the revenue that he can. In New York Poe had already given *Eureka,* his cosmogonic poem, as a lecture, and it had even aroused considerable discussion. Now he had the idea of lecturing in his own region, in Virginia. He intended, as he wrote to Willis, to make a tour in the West and South, and he hoped for assistance from his literary friends and from his old college and West Point acquaintances. Accordingly, he visited the principal cities of Virginia, and Richmond saw once again the man whom it had known when he was young, poor and shabby. All those who had not seen Poe since the days of his obscurity came in crowds to see their distinguished fellow citizen. He appeared handsome, elegant, absolutely correct. I even believe that for some time he had gone so far as to join a temperance society. He chose a theme as broad as it was lofty: *The Poetic Principle,* and he developed it with that lucidity which was one of his gifts. He believed, like the true poet that he was, that the purpose of poetry is of the same nature as its principle, and that it should have no object in view other than itself.

The wonderful reception that he received filled his poor heart with pride and joy; he was so delighted that he spoke of settling down in Richmond and ending his days among the places that his childhood had made dear to him. However, he had some business in New York, and he left on the 4th of October, complaining of weakness and chills. On the evening of the 6th, continuing to feel ill on his arrival in Baltimore, he had his baggage sent to the dock from which he was to leave for Philadelphia, and went into a tavern to get a stimulant. There, unfortunately, he met some old acquaintances and stayed late. The next morning, in the pale shadows of dawn, a corpse was found on the street—should it be put that way?—no, a body still living, but already marked by the royal stamp of Death. On the body, whose name was not known, no papers or money were found, and he was taken to a hospital. It was there that Poe died, Sunday evening October 7, 1849, at the age of 37, defeated by *delirium tremens,* that terrible visitor which had already attacked his mind once or twice. Thus disappeared from the world one of the greatest literary heroes, the man of genius who had written in *The Black Cat* these fateful words: *What disease is like Alcohol!*

This death was almost a suicide,—a suicide prepared for a long time. At least, it caused that kind of scandal. There was a great uproar, and *virtue* gave free rein to its pretentious *cant,* openly and voluptuously. The kindest funeral orations could not avoid the inevitable bourgeois moralizing and were quick to seize such an admirable occasion. Mr. Griswold slandered him; Mr. Willis, sincerely grieved, was more than decent. Alas! the man who had scaled the most arduous heights of esthetics and plunged into the least explored abysses of the human intellect, he who, through a life which resembled an unrelieved tempest, had found new means, unknown techniques to astonish the imagination, to charm minds thirsty for the Beautiful, had just died within a period of a few hours in a hospital bed,—what a fate! So much greatness and so much misfortune, to raise a storm of bourgeois phrases, to become the food and theme of virtuous journalists!

Ut declamatio fias!

Spectacles of this sort are not new; it is rare for the newly buried great not to be subjects of scandal. Moreover, Society does not like these mad wretches, and, whether they disturb its festivities or whether it naïvely regards them as scourges, it is undoubtedly right. Who does not recall the declamations in Paris at the time of Balzac's death, in spite of his perfectly natural end?—And still more recently,—just a year ago today,—when a writer,[10] admirably honest, highly intelligent, and *who was always lucid*, discreetly, without bothering anyone,—so discreetly that his discretion looked like scorn,—went away to free his soul in the darkest street that he could find,—what disgusting homilies!—what refined assassination! A famous journalist, who will never learn generosity from Jesus, thought the event amusing enough to commemorate in a coarse pun.—In the long list of the *rights of man* which the wisdom of the 19th century keeps increasing so often and so complacently, two rather important ones have been forgotten, the right to contradict oneself and the right to take one's leave. But *Society* considers anyone who kills himself as insolent; it would gladly punish the earthly remains, like the unfortunate soldier, stricken with vampirism, who was exasperated to the point of fury by a cadaver.—And nevertheless, it may be said that, in certain circumstances, after a grave consideration of certain incompatibilities, with a firm belief in certain dogmas and transmigrations,—it may be said, without exaggeration and in all seriousness, that suicide is sometimes the most rational act of life.—And thus is formed an already numerous company of phantoms, which haunts us familiarly, and of which each member comes to praise his present repose and to pour out his persuasions.[11]

We must admit, nevertheless, that the lugubrious end of the author of *Eureka* aroused some consoling exceptions, lacking which we would have to despair, and the situation would be unbearable. Mr. Willis, as I have said, spoke honestly and even with emotion of the good relations that he had always had with Poe. John Neal and George Graham recall Mr. Griswold to shame. Longfellow,—who is all the more commendable since Poe had cruelly maltreated him,—praised his great power as a poet and as a prose writer in a manner worthy of a poet. Someone wrote anonymously that literary America had lost its strongest mind. But it was Mrs. Clemm whose heart was broken, torn, and pierced by the seven swords. Edgar was both her son and her daughter. It was a hard destiny, Willis says (from whom I borrow these details almost word for word), a hard destiny that she watched over and protected. For Edgar Poe was a disconcerting man; in addition to the fact that he wrote with painstaking care, and *in a style too much above the average intellectual level to be well paid,* he was always deep in financial trouble, and often he and his ill wife lacked the necessities of life. One day an old, sweet, serious woman came into Willis' office. It was Mrs. Clemm. She was *looking for work* for her dear Edgar. The biographer says that he was singularly struck, not only by her perfect appreciation, her just appraisal of her son-in-law's talents, but also by her whole outer being,—by her sweet and sad voice, by her fine, slightly old-fashioned manners. He adds that for several years he saw this indefatigable servant of genius, poorly and insufficiently dressed, going from office to office in order to sell now a poem, now an article, sometimes saying that *he* was ill,—the sole explanation, the sole reason, the invariable excuse that she gave when her son-in-law was momentarily stricken by one of those periods of sterility that nervous writers know,—never letting a word fall from her lips which could be interpreted as a doubt, as a lessening of confidence in the genius and will of her beloved. When her daughter died, she attached herself to the survivor of the disastrous battle with increased maternal ardor, she lived with him, took care of him, watching over him, defending him against life and against himself. Assuredly, Willis concludes with lofty and just reasoning, if the devotion of a woman, born of a first love and maintained by human passion, glorifies and consecrates its object, what could one not say in support of a man who inspired a devotion like this, pure, disinterested and as holy as a divine sentinel? The detractors of Poe ought to have realized that there are fascinations so powerful that they can only be virtues.

One can guess how terrible the news was for the unhappy woman. Here are some lines from a letter which she wrote to Willis:

"I have this morning heard of the death of my darling Eddie. *** Can you give me any circumstances or particulars? *** Oh! do not desert your poor friend in this bitter affliction. *** Ask Mr. — to come, as I must deliver a message to him from my poor Eddie. *** I need not ask you to notice his death and to speak well of him. I know you will. But say what an affectionate son he was to me, his poor desolate mother. ***"

It seems to me that this woman has more than ancient greatness. Struck by an irreparable blow, she thinks only of the reputation of the person who was everything to her, and she is not content to have it said that he was a genius, it must be known that he was a dutiful and affectionate man. It is clear that his mother,—a torch and hearth illuminated by a ray from heaven,—has been sent as an example to races who are too careless of devotion, of heroism, and of everything that is beyond duty. Was it not just to inscribe above the works of the poet the name of the woman who was the moral sun of his life? He will preserve in his glory the name of the woman whose love was able to care for his wounds, and whose image will ceaselessly hover over the martyrology of literature.

III

The life of Poe, his manners and morals, his physical being, everything that constituted the whole of his personality, appear to us as something at once dark and brilliant. His person was singular, fascinating, and like his works, marked by an indefinable stamp of melancholy. Moreover, he was remarkably gifted in every way. As a young man he had shown an exceptional skill in every kind of physical exercise, and although he was small, with the feet and hands of a woman, although his whole being had a delicate, feminine character, he was more than robust and capable of wonderful feats of strength. When he was a boy he won a bet for an extraordinary demonstration of swimming. One would say that Nature grants an energetic temperament to those from whom it expects great things, just as it gives a powerful vitality to those trees which symbolize grief and sorrow. Such men, sometimes puny in appearance, are cut in an athletic mold, fit for orgies and for work, inclined to excess and capable of extraordinary sobriety.

There are some things about Edgar Poe concerning which agreement is unanimous, as for example, his great natural distinction, his eloquence and his handsome appearance, of which it is said he was a little vain. His manners, a strange mixture of aloofness and exquisite gentleness, were full of assurance. His face, bearing, gestures, the carriage of his head, all marked him, especially in his best years, as an exceptional person. His whole being breathed an air of intense solemnity. He was really singled out by nature, like those passersby who catch the eye of the spectator and remain in his memory. Even the pedantic and bitter Griswold admits that, when he went to visit Poe, whom he found still pale and ill after the sickness and death of his wife, he was very much struck, not only by the perfection of his manners, but also by the aristocratic appearance, the perfumed atmosphere of his apartment, even though it was modestly furnished. Griswold does not realize that, more than anyone else, the poet has the wonderful gift, attributed to Parisian and Spanish women, of being able to adorn himself with nothing, and that Poe, attached to everything that was beautiful, would have found a way to transform a cottage into a new kind of palace. Did he not write, in the most curious and original way, about new conceptions of furniture, about planning country houses, about gardens and reforms in landscape architecture?

There is a charming letter written by Mrs. Frances Osgood, who was one of Poe's friends, and who gives us most interesting details about his manners, his peron and his domestic life. This woman, who was herself a distinguished literary person, courageously denies all the vices and faults attributed to the poet. "With men," she tells Griswold, "perhaps he was as you picture him, and as a man you may be right. I think no one could know him—certainly no woman—without feeling the same interest . . . I have never seen him otherwise than gentle, generous, well bred, and fastidiously refined.

"My first meeting with the poet was at the Astor House. A few days previous Mr. Willis had handed me, at the *table d'hote,* that strange and thrilling poem entitled 'The Raven,' saying that the author wanted my opinion of it. Its effect upon me was so singular, so like that of 'wierd, unearthly music,' that it was with a feeling almost of dread I heard he desired an introduction . . . . With his proud and beautiful head erect, his dark eyes flashing with the elective light of feeling and of thought, a peculiar, and inimitable blending of sweetness and hauteur in his expression and manner, he greeted me, calmly, gravely, almost coldly; yet with so marked an earnestness that I could not help being deeply impressed by it. From that moment until his death we were friends . . . . And in his last words, ere reason had forever left her imperial throne in that overtasked brain, I have a touching memento of his undying faith and friendship.

"It was in his own simple yet poetical home that to me, the character of Edgar Poe appeared in its most beautiful light. Playful, affectionate, witty, alternately docile and wayward as a petted child—for his young, gentle, and idolized wife, and for all who came, he had, even in the midst of his most harassing literary duties, a kind word, a pleasant smile, a graceful and courteous attention. At his desk, beneath the romantic picture of his loved and lost Lenore, he would sit, hour after hour, patient, assiduous, and uncomplaining, tracing, in an exquisitely clear chirography, and with almost superhuman swiftness, the lightning thoughts—the 'rare and radiant' fancies as they flashed through his wonderful and ever-wakeful brain. I recollect one morning, toward the close of his residence in this city, when he seemed unusually gay and light-hearted. Virginia, his sweet wife, had written me a pressing invitation to come to them; and I, who could never resist her affectionate summons . . . found him just completing his series of papers, entitled 'The Literati of New York.' 'See,' said he, displaying in triumph several little rolls of narrow papers (he always wrote thus for the press), 'I am going to show you, by the difference of length in these, the different degrees of estimation in which I hold all you literary people. In each of these one of you is rolled up and fully discussd. Come, Virginia, help me.' And one by one they unfolded them. At last they came to one which seemed interminable. Virginia laughingly ran to one corner of the room with one end, and her husband to the opposite with the other. 'And whose lengthened sweetness long drawn out is that?' said I. 'Hear her!' he cried, 'just as if her little vain heart didn't tell her it's herself.' "

"During that year, while travelling for my health, I maintained a correspondence with Mr. Poe, in accordance with the earnest entreaties of his wife, who imagined that my influence over him had a restraining and beneficial effect . . . of the charming love and confidence that existed between his wife and himself, always delightfully apparent to me, in spite of the many little poetical episodes, in which the impassioned romance of his temperament impelled him to indulge; of this I cannot speak too earnestly—too warmly. I believe she was the only woman whom he ever truly loved . . . ."[12]

Love never figures in Poe's stories. At least, *Ligeia,* and *Eleanora,* are not love stories, properly speaking, since the central idea on which the work pivots is something quite different. Perhaps he believed that prose was not a language equal to that strange and almost untranslatable sentiment; for his poems, in contrast, are strongly saturated with it. In them the divine passion appears with all its magnificence, like the starry sky, yet always veiled by an irremediable melancholy. Sometimes he speaks of love in his essays, and even as if it were something whose name makes his pen tremble.

In *The Domain of Arnheim,* he declares that the four fundamental conditions of happiness are: life in the open air, *the love of a woman,* detachment from all ambition and the creation of a new Beauty.—What corroborates the idea of Mrs. Frances Osgood about Poe's chivalric respect for women is the fact that, in spite of his prodigious talent for the grotesque and the horrible, there is not a single passage in all his work which has to do with lust or even with sensual pleasures. His portraits of women are, so to speak, aureoled; they shine in the midst of a supernatural atmosphere and are painted with the emphatic touch of a worshiper.—As for the *minor romantic episodes,* is it at all surprising that such a high-strung person, whose chief trait was perhaps a thirst for the Beautiful, should sometimes have passionately cultivated gallantry, that volcanic and musk-scented flower for which the seething minds of poets is the natural soil?

I believe that it is possible to get some idea of his strange personal beauty, mentioned in several biographies, by calling up all the vague but nevertheless characteristic notions contained in the word romantic, a word which is generally used to represent the kinds of beauty in which expression is of paramount importance. Poe had a broad, dominating forehead in which certain protuberances revealed the abundant faculties which they are supposed to represent,[13]—construction, comparison, causality,—and where was enthroned in calm pride the sense of the ideal, the esthetic sense par excellence. Nevertheless, in spite of these gifts, or even because of these disproportionate favors, his head, seen in profile, did not have perhaps an agreeable appearance. As with all things that are excessive in one direction, deficiency can result from abundance, poverty can spring from encroachment. He had large eyes, at once somber and full of light, dark and uncertain in color, tending toward violet, a solid and noble nose, a fine, sad mouth, though slightly smiling, a dark complexion, a pale face, in appearance a little absent-minded and imperceptibly suffused by habitual melancholy.

His conversation was quite remarkable and essentially learned. He was not what is called a glib speaker, —a horrible thing,—and besides his speech, like his pen, had a horror of the conventional; but vast knowledge, powerful language, serious studies, impressions gathered in several countries made his talk instructive. His eloquence, essentially poetic, full of method, and yet operating outside of all known methods, an arsenal of images drawn from a world little frequented by average minds, a prodigious art of deriving from an evident and absolutely acceptable proposition new and secret perceptions, of opening astonishing perspectives, and in a word, the art of delighting, of stimulating thoughts and dreams, of snatching souls out of the mire of routine, such were the dazzling faculties which many persons remember. But sometimes it happened,—so it is said,—that the poet, enjoying a destructive caprice, brusquely brought his friends back to earth with a painful cynicism and brutally demolished the spiritual work which he had just constructed. Something else to note, moreover, is the fact that he was not at all particular about his auditors, and I believe that the reader will have no difficulty in finding other great and original intelligences in history who were at home in any company. Certain minds, solitary in the midst of crowds, and nourishing themselves on monologues, cannot be particular about their audience. In short, it is a kind of fraternity based on scorn.

As for his drunkenness,—publicized and censured with an insistence which could make it appear that all the writers of the United States, except Poe, are angels of sobriety,—something should be said. Several explanations are plausible, and none excludes the others. Above all it must be noted that Willis and Mrs. Osgood emphasize how much his whole constitution was upset by a very small amount of alcohol. Moreover, it is easy to understand why such a truly solitary man, profoundly unhappy, who must often have regarded the whole social system as a paradox and a fraud, a man who, harassed by a pitiless destiny, often said that society was nothing but a mob of wretches (Griswold reports this, scandalized as a man who may think the same thing, but who will never say it),—it is natural, I say, to understand why this poet, cast into the hazards of an undisciplined life while still a child, his mind circumscribed by hard and continuous work, should sometimes have sought the pleasure of forgetfulness in intoxication. Literary rancors, the intoxication of the infinite, domestic problems, the indignities of poverty, all of these Poe fled in the blackness of drunkenness as if in a preparatory tomb. But however good this explanation may seem, I do not consider it sufficiently broad, and I am suspicious of it because of its deplorable simplicity.

I am informed that he did not drink as an epicure, but barbarously, with a speed and dispatch altogether American, as if he were performing a homicidal function, as if he had to kill *something* inside of him, a worm that would not die. It is said, further, that one day, when he was about to remarry (the banns had been published, and as he was being congratulated on a marriage which opened the prospect of the greatest happiness and well-being, he had said: you may have seen the banns, but you may be sure I shall not marry), he went about, frightfully drunk, scandalizing the neighbors of his future wife, thus having recourse to his vice in order to shake off a broken promise made to his poor dead wife whose image was always with him, and about whom he had written so well in his *Annabel Lee.* I believe, then, that in many cases the important fact of premeditation has been clearly established.

Furthermore, in a long article in the *Southern Literary Messenger,*—the magazine whose fortune he had started,—I read that this terrible vice never affected the purity or the finish of his style, the lucidity of his thought or his habit of hard work; that the composition of most of his excellent pieces preceded or followed one of his crises; that after the publication of *Eureka* he let himself go very badly, and that in New York, on the very morning that *The Raven* appeared, while everyone was still talking about him, he staggered conspicuously down Broadway. Notice that the words *preceded or followed* imply that drunkenness could be a stimulant as well as a relaxation.

Now there can be no doubt that—like those fleeting and striking impressions, the more striking in their recurrences as they are more fleeting, which sometimes follow an exterior stimulus, a kind of signal such as the sound of a bell, a musical note, or a forgotten perfume, and which themselves are followed by an event similar to an event already known, which occupied the same place in a previously revealed chain,—like those strange periodic dreams which frequent our sleep,—there exist in drunkeness not only chains of dreams, but sequences of reasonings which, to be reproduced, require the setting in which they were born.[14] If the reader has not been horrified, he has already guessed my conclusion: I believe that often, though certainly not always, Poe's drunkenness was a mnemonic means, a method of work, drastic and fatal, but adapted to his passionate nature. The poet had learned to drink, just as a careful writer takes pains to keep notes. He could not resist the desire to recapture the marvelous or frightening visions, the subtle conceptions which he had experienced in a previous exaltation; they were old acquaintances which attracted him imperiously, and in order to renew contact with them, he took the shortest, but the most dangerous road. What killed him is a part of that which gives us enjoyment today.

IV

I have little to say about the works of this singular genius; the public will show by its response what it thinks of them. It would be difficult for me perhaps, but not impossible, to disentangle his method, to explain his technique, especially in that portion of his work whose principal effect lies in a well handled analysis. I could introduce the reader to the mysteries of his workmanship, speak at length about that aspect of American genius which makes him delight in a difficulty overcome, an enigma explained, a successful *tour de force*,—which leads him to play, with a childish and almost perverse pleasure, in a world of probabilities and conjectures, and to create the hoaxes which his subtle art has made seem plausible. No one will deny that Poe is a marvelous jongleur, and yet I know that he attached the greatest importance to another aspect of his work. I have some more important, though brief, remarks to make.

It is not by these material miracles, which nevertheless have made his reputation, that he will win the admiration of thinking people, it is by his love of the beautiful, by his knowledge of the harmonic conditions of beauty, by his profound and plaintive poetry, carefully wrought, correct and as transparent as a crystal jewel,—by his admirable style, pure and bizarre,—as closely woven as the mesh of chain mail—flexible and painstaking,—whose slightest intention serves to lead the reader gently toward the desired effect,—finally and above all by his very special genius, by that unique temperament which allowed him to picture and to explain the *exceptional case in the moral order* in an impeccable, gripping and terrible manner.—Diderot, to take one example among a hundred, is a sanguine author; Poe is a writer who is all nerves, and even something more,—and the best one I know.

In his case every introductory passage has a quiet drawing power, like a whirlpool. His solemnity surprises the reader and keeps his mind on the alert. Immediately he feels that something serious is involved. And slowly, little by little, a story unfolds whose interest depends on an imperceptible intellectual deviation, on a bold hypothesis, on an unbalanced dose of Nature in the amalgam of faculties. The reader, seized by a kind of vertigo, is constrained to follow the author through his compelling deductions.

No one, I repeat, has told about the *exceptions* in human life and in nature with more magic,—the enthusiastic curiosities of convalescence; the dying seasons charged with enervating splendors, hot, humid and misty weather, when the south wind softens and relaxes one's nerves like the strings of an instrument, when one's eyes fill with tears which do not come from the heart;—hallucinations, first appearing doubtful, then convincing and as rational as a book; the absurd establishing itself in one's mind and controlling it with a frightful logic; hysteria usurping the place of the will, contradiction set up between the nerves and the mind, and personality so out of joint that it expresses grief by a laugh. He analyzes whatever is most fugitive, he weighs the imponderable and describes, in a detailed and scientific manner the effects of which are terrible, all that imaginary world which floats around a high-strung man and leads him into evil.

The fervor with which he throws himself into the grotesque out of love for the grotesque and into the horrible out of love for the horrible serves to verify the sincerity of his work, and the harmony between the man and the poet.—I have already pointed out that, in certain men, this fervor was often the result of a vast, unemployed vital energy, sometimes the result of a stubborn chastity, and also of a profound dammed-up sensibility. The unnatural pleasure that a man may feel in watching the flow of his own blood, sudden violent, useless movements, cries uttered for no reason at all, are phenomena of the same kind.

In the midst of the rarefied air of this literature, the mind may feel the vague anguish, the fear close to tears and the uneasiness of heart which exist in vast and strange places. But admiration prevails, and the art is so great! The backgrounds and accessories are appropriate to the feelings of the persons involved. Solitude of nature or agitation of cities, everything is described energetically and fantastically. Like our own Eugene Delacroix,[15] who has raised his art to the level of great poetry, Edgar Poe loves to represent agitated figures against violet or greenish backgrounds in which are revealed the phosphorescence of decay and the smell of storms. So-called inanimate Nature takes on the nature of living beings, and, like them, shudders with a supernatural and convulsive shudder. Opium deepens the feeling of space; opium gives a magical feeling to all tones, and makes all sounds vibrate with a more sonorous significance. Sometimes magnificent vistas, saturated with light and color, suddenly open up in his landscapes, and in the distance are seen oriental cities and buildings, etherealized by the distance, bathed in a golden sunlight.

The characters in Poe, or rather the character in Poe, the man with excessively acute faculties, the man with relaxed nerves, the man whose patient and ardent will hurls defiance at difficulties, he whose gaze is fixed as straight as a sword on objects which increase in importance under his gaze,—this man is Poe himself.—And his women, all luminous and sickly, dying of strange diseases, and speaking with a voice which is like music, they are also Poe; or at least, through their strange aspirations, through their knowledge, through their incurable melancholy, they strongly share the nature of their creator. As for his ideal woman, his Titanide, she is revealed in several portraits scattered through his sparse collection of poems, portraits, or rather ways of feeling beauty, which the temperament of the author joins and fuses in a vague but perceptible unity, and in which exists perhaps more delicately than elsewhere that insatiable love of the Beautiful, which is his great title of respect, that is the summation of his claims on the affection and admiration of poets.

Under the title: *Histoires Extraordinaires* we have gathered together various stories chosen from the whole of Poe's work. His work comprises a considerable number of short stories, an equal quantity of critical and miscellaneous articles, a philosophical poem *(Eureka)*, poems, and a purely realistic novel *(The Narrative of Arthur Gordon Pym)*.

If, as I hope, I should have occasion to speak further of this poet, I shall give an analysis of his philosophical and literary ideas, and in general of works whose complete translation would have little chance of success with a public which much prefers amusement and emotion to the most important philosophical truth.

Notes Nouvelles Sur

Edgar Poe: 1857

*Littérature de décadence!—Paroles vides que nous entendons souvent tomber, avec la sonorité d'un bâillement emphatique, de la bouche de ces sphinx sans énigme qui veillent devant les portes saintes de l'Esthétique classique. A chaque fois que l'irréfutable oracle retentit, on peut affirmer qu'il s'agit d'un ouvrage plus amusant que l'*ILIADE. *Il est évidemment question d'un poème ou d'un roman dont toutes les parties sont habilement disposées pour la surprise, dont le style est magnifiquement orné, où toutes les ressources du langage et de la prosodie sont utilisées par une main impeccable. Lorsque j'entends ronfler l'anathème,—qui, pour le dire en passant, tombe généralement sur quelque poète préféré,—je suis toujours saisi de l'envie de répondre Me prenez-vous pour un barbare comme vous, et me croyez-vous capable de me divertir aussi tristement que vous faites? Des comparaisons grotesques s'agitent alors dans mon cerveau; il me semble que deux femmes me sont présentées: l'une, matrone rustique, répugnante de santé et de vertu, sans allure et sans regard, bref,* NE DEVANT RIEN QU'A LA SIMPLE

NEW NOTES ON EDGAR POE: 1857

I

Decadent literature!—Empty words which we often hear fall, with the sonority of a deep yawn, from the mouths of those unenigmatic sphinxes who keep watch before the sacred doors of classical Esthetics. Each time that the irrefutable oracle resounds, one can be sure that it is about a work more amusing than the *Iliad.* It is evidently a question of a poem or of a novel all of whose parts are skillfully designed for surprise, whose style is magnificently embellished, where all the resources of language and prosody are utilized by an impeccable hand. When I hear the anathema boom out, —which, I might say in passing, usually falls on some favorite poet,—I am always seized with the desire to reply: Do you take me for a barbarian like you and do you believe me capable of amusing myself as dismally as you do? Then grotesque comparisons stir in my brain; it seems to me that two women appear before me: one, a rustic matron, repugnant in her health and virtue, plain and expressionless, in short, *owing everything to simple nature;* the other, one of those beauties who dominate and oppress one's memory, adding all the eloquence of dress to her profound and original charm, well poised, conscious and queen of herself,—with a speaking voice like a well-tuned instrument, and eyes laden with thoughts, but revealing only what they wish. I would not hesitate in my choice, and yet there are pedagogical sphinxes who would reproach me for my failure to respect classical honor.—But, putting aside parables, I think it is permissible to ask these wise men if they really understand all the vanity, all the futility of their wisdom. The phrase *decadent literature* implies that there is a scale of literatures, an infantile, a childish, an adolescent, etc. This term, in other words, supposes something fatal and providential, like an ineluctable decree; and it is altogether unfair to reproach us for fulfilling the mysterious law. All that I can understand in this academic phrase is that it is shameful to obey this law with pleasure and that we are guilty to rejoice in our destiny.—The sun, which a few hours ago overwhelmed everything with its direct white light, is soon going to flood the western horizon with variegated colors. In the play of light of the dying sun certain poetic spirits will find new delights; they will discover there dazzling colonnades, cascades of molten metal, paradises of fire, a sad splendor, the pleasure of regret, all the magic of dreams, all the memories of opium. And indeed the sunset will appear to them like the marvelous allegory of a soul filled with life which descends behind the horizon with a magnificent store of thoughts and dreams.

But what the narrow-minded professors have not realized is that, in the movement of life, there may occur some complication, some combination quite unforeseen by their schoolboy wisdom. And then their inadequate language fails, as in the case—a phenomenon which perhaps will increase with variants—of a nation which begins with decadence and thus starts where others end.

Let new literatures develop among the immense colonies of the present century and there will result most certainly spiritual accidents of a nature disturbing to the academic mind. Young and old at the same time, America babbles and rambles with an astonishing volubility. Who could count its poets? They are innumerable. Its *blue stockings?* They clutter the magazines. Its critics? You may be sure that they have pedants who are as good as ours at constantly recalling the artist to ancient beauty, at questioning a poet or a novelist on the morality of his purpose and the merit of his intentions. There can be found there as here, but even more than here, men of letters who do not know how to spell; a childish, useless activity; compilers in abundance, hack writers, plagiarists of plagiaries, and critics of critics. In this maelström of mediocrity, in this society enamored of material perfections,—a new kind of scandal which makes intelligible the grandeur of inactive peoples,—in this society eager for surprises, in love with life, but especially with a life full of excitements, a man has appeared who was great not only in his metaphysical subtlety, in the sinister or bewitching beauty of his conceptions, in the rigor of his analysis, but also great and not less great as a *caricature.* —I must explain myself with some care; for recently a rash critic, in order to disparage Edgar Poe and to invalidate the sincerity of my admiration, used the word *jongleur* which I myself had applied to the noble poet as a sort of praise.

From the midst of a greedy world, hungry for material things, Poe took flight in dreams. Stifled as he was by the American atmosphere, he wrote at the beginning of *Eureka:* "I offer this book to those who have put faith in dreams as in the only realities!" He was in himself an admirable protest, and he made his protest in his own particular way. The author who, in *The Colloquy of Monos and Una,* pours out his scorn and disgust for democracy, progress and *civilization,* this author is the same one who, in order to encourage credulity, to delight the stupidity of his contemporaries, has stressed human sovereignty most emphatically and has very ingeniously fabricated hoaxes flattering to the pride of *modern man.* Considered in this light, Poe seems like a helot who wishes to make his master blush. Finally, to state my thought even more clearly, Poe was always great not only in his noble conceptions, but also as a prankster.

II

For he was never a dupe! I do not think that the Virginian who calmly wrote in the midst of a rising tide of democracy: "People have nothing to do with laws except to obey them," has ever been a victim of modern wisdom; and: "The nose of a mob is its imagination. By this, at any time, it can be quietly led."—and a hundred other passages in which mockery falls thick and fast like a hail of bullets, but still remains proud and indifferent.—The Swedenborgians congratulate him on his *Mesmeric Revelation,* like those naïve Illuminati who formerly hailed in the author of the *Diable amoureux*[1] a discoverer of their mysteries; they thank him for the great truths which he has just proclaimed,—for they have discovered (O verifiers of the unverifiable!) that all that which he has set forth is absolutely true; —although, at first, these good people confess, they had suspected that it might well have been merely fictitious. Poe answers that, so far as he is concerned, he has never doubted it.—Must I cite in addition this short passage which catches my eye while scanning for the hundredth times his amusing *Marginalia,* which are the secret chambers, as it were, of his mind: "The enormous multiplication of books in all branches of knowledge is one of the greatest scourges of this age, for it is one of the most serious obstacles to the acquisition of all positive knowledge." Aristocrat by nature even more than by birth, the Virginian, the Southerner, the Byron gone astray in a bad world, has always kept his philosophic impassibility and, whether he defines the nose of the mob, whether he mocks the fabricators of religions, whether he scoffs at libraries, he remains what the true poet was and always will be,—a truth clothed in a strange manner, an apparent paradox, who does not wish to be elbowed by the crowd and who runs to the far east when the fireworks go off in the west.

But more important than anything else: we shall see that this author, product of a century infatuated with itself, child of a nation more infatuated with itself than all others, has clearly seen, has imperturbably affirmed the natural wickedness of man. There is in man, he says, a mysterious force which modern philosophy does not wish to take into consideration; nevertheless, without this nameless force, without this primordial bent, a host of human actions will remain unexplained, inexplicable. These actions are attractive only *because* they are bad, dangerous; they possess the fascination of the abyss. This primitive, irresistible force is natural Perversity, which makes man constantly and simultaneously a murderer and a suicide, an assassin and a hangman; —for he adds, with a remarkably satanic sublety, the impossibility of finding a reasonably sufficient motive for certain wicked and perilous actions could lead us to consider them as the result of the suggestions of the Devil, if experience and history did not teach us that God often draws from them the establishment of order and the punishment of scoundrels;—*after having used the same scoundrels as accomplices!* such is the thought which, I confess, slips into my mind, an implication as inevitable as it is perfidious. But for the present I wish to consider only the great forgotten truth,—the primordial perversity of man,—and it is not without a certain satisfaction that I see some vestiges of ancient wisdom return to us from a country from which we did not expect them. It is pleasant to know that some fragments of an old truth are exploded in the faces of all these obsequious flatterers of humanity, of all these humbugs and quacks who repeat in every possible tone of voice: "I am born good, and you too, and all of us are born good!" forgetting, no! pretending to forget, like misguided equalitarians, that we are all born marked for evil!

Of what lies could he be a dupe, he who sometimes —sad necessity of his environment—dealt with them so well? What scorn for pseudo-philosophy on his good days, on the days when he was, so to speak, inspired! This poet, several of whose compositions seem deliberately made to confirm the alleged omnipotence of man, has sometimes wished to purge himself. The day that he wrote: "All certainty is in dreams," he thrust back his own Americanism into the region of inferior things; at other times, becoming again the true poet, doubtless obeying the ineluctable truth which haunts us like a demon, he uttered the ardent sighs of *the fallen angel who remembers heaven;* he lamented the golden age and the lost Eden; he wept over all the magnificence of nature *shrivelling up before the hot breath of fiery furnaces;* finally, he produced those admirable pages: *The Colloquy of Monos and Una* which would have charmed and troubled the impeccable De Maistre.

It is he who said about socialism at a time when the latter did not yet have a name, or when, at least, this name was not completely popularized: "The world is infested, just now, by a new sect of philosophers, who have not yet suspected themselves of forming a sect, and who, consequently, have adopted no name. They are the *Believers in everything Old.* Their High Priest in the East, is Charles Fourier,—in the West, Horace Greeley; and high priests they are to some purpose. The only common bond among the sect is Credulity:—let us call it Insanity at once, and be done with it. Ask any one of them *why* he believes this or that, and, if he be conscientious, (ignorant people usually are,) he will make you very much such a reply as Talleyrand made when asked why he believed in the Bible. 'I believe in it first,' said he, 'because I am Bishop of Autun; and, secondly, *because I know nothing about it at all.*' What these philosophers call 'argument' is a way they have '*de nier ce qui est et d'expliquer ce qui n'est pas.*' "[2]

Progress, that great heresy of decay, likewise could not escape him. The reader will see in different passages what terms he used to characterize it. One could truly say, considering the fervor that he expends, that he had to vent his spleen on it, as on a public nuisance or as on a pest in the street. How he would have laughed, with the poet's scornful laugh, which alienates simpletons, had he happened, as I did, upon this wonderful statement which reminds one of the ridiculous and deliberate absurdities of clowns. I discovered it treacherously blazoned in an eminently serious magazine:—*The unceasing progress of science has very recently made possible the rediscovery of the lost and long sought secret of . . .* (Greek fire, the tempering of copper, something or other which has vanished), *of which the most successful applications date back to a* barbarous *and very old period!!!* That is a sentence which can be called a real find, a brilliant discovery, even in a century of *unceasing progress;* but I believe that the mummy Allamistakeo[3] would not have failed to ask with a gentle and discreet tone of superiority, if it were also thanks to *unceasing* progress,—to the fatal, irresistible law of progress,—that this famous secret had been lost.—Moreover, to become serious about a subject which is as sad as it is laughable, is it not a really stupefying thing to see a nation, several nations, and presently all humanity, say to its wise men, its magicians: I shall love you and I shall make you great if you convince me that we are progressing unconsciously, inevitably,—while sleeping; rid us of responsibility, veil for us the humiliation of comparisons, turn history into sophistries and you will be able to call yourselves the wisest of the wise? Is it not a cause for astonishment that this simple idea does not flash into everyone's mind: that progress (in so far as there is progress) perfects sorrow to the same extent that it refines pleasure and that, if the epidermis of peoples is becoming delicate, they are evidently pursuing only an *Italiam fugientem,* a conquest lost every minute, a progress always negating itself?

But these illusions which, it must be added, are selfish, originate in a foundation of perversity and falsehood,—meteors rising from swamps,—which fill with disdain souls in love with the eternal fire, like Edgar Poe, and exasperate foggy minds like Jean-Jacques Rousseau, in whom a wounded and rebellious sensibility takes the place of philosophy. That he was justified in his attack on the *depraved animal* is undeniable; but the depraved animal has the right to reproach him for invoking simple nature. Nature produces only monsters, and the whole question is to understand the word *savages.* No philosopher will dare to propose as models those wretched, rotten hordes, victims of the elements, prey of the animals, as incapable of manufacturing arms as of conceiving the idea of a spiritual and supreme power. But, if one wishes to compare modern man, civilized man, with the savage, or rather a so-called civilized nation with a so-called savage nation, that is to say one deprived of all the ingenious inventions which absolve the individual of heroism, who does not see that all honor goes to the savage? By his nature, by very necessity itself, he is encyclopedic, while civilized man finds himself confined to the infinitely small regions of specialization. Civilized man invents the philosophy of progress to console himself for his abdication and for his downfall; while the savage man, redoubtable and respected husband, warrior forced to personal bravery, poet in the melancholy hours when the setting sun inspires songs of the past and of his forefathers, skirts more closely the edge of the ideal. Of what lack shall we dare accuse him ? He has the priest, he has the magician and the doctor. What am I saying?

He has the dandy, supreme incarnation of the idea of the beautiful given expression in material life, he who dictates form and governs manners. His clothing, his adornments, his weapons, his pipe give proof of an inventive faculty which for a long time has deserted us. Shall we compare our sluggish eyes and our deafened ears to those eyes which pierce the mist, to those ears *which would hear the grass growing?* And the savage woman with a simple and childlike soul, an obedient and winning animal, giving herself entirely and knowing that she is only half of a destiny, shall we declare her inferior to the American woman whom M. Bellegarique (editor of the *Grocer's Bulletin!)* thought he was praising by saying that she was the ideal of the kept woman? This same woman, whose over-practical manners inspired Edgar Poe, he who was so gallant, so respectful of beauty, to write the following sad lines: "The frightfully long money-pouches—'like the Cucumber called the Gigantic'—which have come in vogue among our belles—are *not* of Parisian origin, as many suppose, but are strictly indigenous here. The fact is, such a fashion would be quite out of place in Paris, where it is money *only* that women keep in a purse. The purse of an American lady, however, must be large enough to carry both her money and the soul of its owner."[4] As for religion, I shall not speak of Vitzilipoutzli as lightly as Alfred de Musset has done; I confess without shame that I much prefer the cult of Teutatès to that of Mammon; and the priest who offers to the cruel extorter of human sacrifices victims who die *honorably*, victims who *wish* to die, seems to me a quite sweet and human being compared to the financier who immolates whole populations solely in his own interest. Now and then, these matters are still understood, and I once found in an article by M. Barbey d'Aurevilly an exclamation of philosophic sadness which sums up everything that I should like to say about the subject: "Civilized peoples, who keep casting stones at savages, soon you will not deserve to be even idolaters!"

Such an environment,—although I have already said so, I cannot resist the desire to repeat it,—is hardly made for poets. What a French mind, even the most democratic, understands by a State, would find no place in an American mind. For every intellect of the old world, a political State has a center of movement which is its brain and its sun, old and glorious memories, long poetic and military annals, an aristocracy to which poverty, daughter of revolutions, can add only a paradoxical luster; but That! that mob of buyers and sellers, that nameless creature, that headless monster, that outcast on the other side of the ocean, you call that a State!—I agree, if a vast tavern where the customer crowds in and conducts his business on dirty tables, amid the din of coarse speech, can be compared to a *salon*, to what we formerly called a salon, a republic of the mind presided over by beauty!

It will always be difficult to exercise, both nobly and fruitfully, the profession of a man of letters, without being exposed to defamation, to the slander of the impotent, to the envy of the rich,—that envy which is their punishment!—to the vengeance of bourgeois mediocrity. But what is difficult in a limited monarchy or in an ordinary republic becomes almost impracticable in a sort of Capernaum where each policeman of public opinion keeps order in the interest of his vices,—or of his virtues, for it is all one and the same thing;—where a poet, a novelist of a country in which slavery exists, is a detestable writer in the eyes of an abolitionist critic; where one does not know which is more scandalous,—the disorder of cynicism or the imperturbability of Biblical hypocrisy. To burn chained Negroes guilty of having felt their black cheeks sting with the blush of honor, to play with guns in the pit of a theater, to establish polygamy in the paradises of the West, which the savages (this term seems unjust) had not yet soiled with these shameful utopias, to post on walls, doubtless to sanctify the principle of unlimited liberty, *the cure for nine months' illnesses,* such are some of the salient characteristics, some of the moral examples of the noble country of Franklin, the inventor of a counting-house morality, the hero of a century devoted to materialism. It is good to consider constantly these extraordinary examples of gross behavior in a time when americanomania has become almost a fashionable passion, to the extent that an archbishop has been able to promise us quite seriously that Providence would soon call us to enjoy this transatlantic ideal.

III

Such a social environment necessarily engenders corresponding literary errors. Poe reacted against these errors as often as he could, and with all his might. We must not be surprised then that American writers, while recognizing his singular power as a poet and as a storyteller, have always tended to question his ability as a critic. In a country where the idea of utility, the most hostile in the world to the idea of beauty, dominates and takes precedence over everything, the perfect critic will be the most *respectable,* that is to say the one whose tendencies and desires will best approximate the tendencies and desires of his public,—the one who, confusing the intellectual faculties of the writer and the categories of writing, will assign to all a single goal,—the one who will seek in a book of poetry the means of perfecting conscience. Naturally he will become all the less concerned with the real, the positive beauties of poetry; he will be all the less shocked by imperfections and even by faults in execution. Edgar Poe, on the contrary, dividing the world of the mind into *pure Intellect, Taste,* and *moral Sense,* applied criticism in accordance with the category to which the object of his analysis belonged. He was above all sensitive to perfection of plan and to correctness of execution; taking apart literary works like defective pieces of machinery (considering the goal that they wished to attain), noting carefully the flaws of workmanship; and when he passed to the detail of the work, to its plastic expression, in a word, to style, examining meticulously and without omissions the faults of prosody, the grammatical errors and all the mass of dross which, among writers who are not artists, besmirch the best intentions and deform the most noble conceptions.

For him, Imagination is the queen of faculties; but by this word he understands something greater than that which is understood by the average reader. Imagination is not fantasy; nor is it sensibility, although it may be difficult to conceive of an imaginative man who would be lacking in sensibility. Imagination is an almost divine faculty which perceives immediately and without philosophical methods the inner and secret relations of things, the correspondences and the analogies. The honors and functions which he grants to this faculty give it such value (at least when the thought of the author has been well understood) that a scholar without imagination appears only as a pseudo-scholar, or at least as an incomplete scholar.

Among the literary domains where imagination can obtain the most curious results, can harvest treasures, not the richest, the most precious (those belong to poetry), but the most numerous and the most varied, there is one of which Poe is especially fond; it is the *Short Story*. It has the immense advantage over the novel of vast proportions that its brevity adds to the intensity of effect. This type of reading, which can be accomplished in one sitting, leaves in the mind a more powerful impression than a broken reading, often interrupted by the worries of business and the cares of social life. The unity of impression, the totality of effect is an immense advantage which can give to this type of composition a very special superiority, to such an extent that an extremely short story (which is doubtless a fault) is even better than an extremely long story. The artist, if he is skillful, will not adapt his thoughts to the incidents, but, having conceived deliberately and at leisure an effect to be produced, will invent the incidents, will combine the events most suitable to bring about the desired effect. If the first sentence is not written with the idea of preparing this final impression, the work has failed from the start. There must not creep into the entire composition a single word which is not intentional, which does not tend, directly or indirectly, to complete the premeditated design.

There is one point in which the short story is superior even to the poem. Rhythm is necessary to the development of the idea of beauty, which is the greatest and the most noble aim of poetry. Now, the artifices of rhythm are an insurmountable obstacle to the minute development of thought and expression which has *truth* as its object. For truth can often be the goal of the short story, and reasoning the best tool for the construction of a perfect short story. That is why this type of composition, which is not as high in the scale as pure poetry, can provide more varied results, more easily appreciated by the average reader. Moreover, the author of a short story has at his disposal a multitude of tones, of nuances of language, the rational tone, the sarcastic, the humorous, which are repudiated by poetry and which are, as it were, dissonances, outrages to the idea of pure beauty. And that is also why the author who seeks in the short story the single goal of beauty works only at a great disadvantage, deprived as he is of the most useful instrument, rhythm. I know that in all literatures efforts have been made, often successful, to create purely poetic short stories; Edgar Poe himself has written some very beautiful ones. But they are struggles and efforts which serve only to prove the strength of the true means adapted to the corresponding goals, and I am inclined to believe that in the case of some authors, the greatest that can be chosen, these heroic attempts spring from despair.

IV

"That poets (using the word comprehensively, as including artists in general) are a *genus irritabile,* is well understood; but the *why,* seems not to be commonly seen. An artist *is* an artist only by dint of his exquisite sense of Beauty—a sense affording him rapturous enjoyment, but at the same time implying, or involving, an equally exquisite sense of Deformity or disproportion. Thus a wrong—an injustice—done a poet who is really a poet, excites him to a degree which, to ordinary apprehension, appears disproportionate with the wrong. Poets *see* injustice—*never* where it does not exist—but very often where the unpoetical see no injustice whatever. Thus the poetical irritability has no reference to 'temper' in the vulgar sense, but merely to a more than usual clear-sightedness in respect to Wrong:—this clear-sightedness being nothing more than a corollary from the vivid perception of Right—of justice—of proportion—in a word, of the beautiful. But one thing is clear—that the man who is *not* 'irritable,' (to the ordinary apprehension), is *no poet.*"[5]

Thus the poet himself speaks, preparing an excellent and irrefutable apologia for all those of his race. Poe carried this sensibility into his literary affairs, and the extreme importance which he attached to things poetic often led him to use a tone in which, according to the judgment of the weak, a feeling of superiority became too evident. I have already mentioned, I believe, that several prejudices which he had to combat, false ideas, commonplace opinions which circulated around him, have for a long time infected the French press. It will not be useless then to give a brief account of some of his most important opinions relative to poetic composition. The parallelism of error will make their application quite easy.

But above all, I must point out that in addition to the share which Poe granted to a natural, innate poetic gift, he gave an importance to knowledge, work, and analysis that will seem excessive to arrogant and unlettered persons. Not only has he expended considerable efforts to subject to his will the fleeting spirit of happy moments, in order to recall at will those exquisite sensations, those spiritual longings, those states of poetic health, so rare and so precious that they could truly be considered as graces exterior to man and as visitations; but also he has subjected inspiration to method, to the most severe analysis. The choice of means! he returns to that constantly, he insists with a learned eloquence upon the adjustment of means to effect, on the use of rime, on the perfecting of the refrain, on the adaptation of rhythm to feeling. He maintained that he who cannot seize the intangible is not a poet; that he alone is a poet who is master of his memory, the sovereign of words, the record book of his own feelings always open for examination. Everything for the conclusion! he often repeats. Even a sonnet needs a plan, and the construction, the armature, so to speak, is the most important guarantee of the mysterious life of works of the mind.

I turn naturally to the article entitled *The Poetic Principle*, and I find from the very beginning a vigorous protest against what could be called, in the field of poetry, the heresy of length or of dimension,—the absurd importance attributed to bulky poems. "I hold that a long poem does not exist. I maintain that the phrase, 'a long poem,' is simply a flat contradiction in terms." In fact, a poem deserves its title only insomuch as it excites and uplifts the soul, and the real merit of a poem is due to this excitation, to this *uplifting* of the soul. But, from psychological necessity, all these excitations are fugitive and transitory. This strange mood into which the soul of the reader has been drawn by force, as it were, will certainly not last as long as the reading of a poem which exceeds human capacity for enthusiasm.

It is obvious then that the epic poem stands condemned. For a work of that length can be considered poetic only insofar as one sacrifices the vital condition of every work of art, Unity;—I do not mean unity in the conception, but unity in the impression, the *totality* of effect, as I said when I had occasion to compare the novel with the short story. The epic poem then appears to us, esthetically speaking, as a paradox. It is possible that by-gone ages have produced a series of lyric poems, later compiled into epic poems; but every *epic intention* obviously is the result of an imperfect sense of art. The time for these artistic anomalies has passed, and it is even very doubtful that a long poem has ever been truly popular in the full meaning of the word.

It must be added that a too short poem, one which does not furnish a *pabulum* that will sustain the excitation created, one which is not equal to the natural appetite of the reader, is also very defective. However brilliant and intense the effect may be, it is not lasting; memory does not retain it; it is like a seal, which placed too lightly and too hastily, has not had time to imprint its image on the wax.

But there is another heresy which, thanks to the hypocrisy, to the dullness, and to the baseness of human minds, is even more formidable and has a greater chance of survival,—an error which has a hardier life, —I wish to speak of the heresy of *teaching a lesson* which includes as inevitable corollaries the heresy of *passion*, of *truth*, and of *morality*. A great many people imagine that the aim of poetry is a lesson of some sort, that it must now fortify the conscience, now perfect morals, now in short *prove* something or other which is useful. Edgar Poe claims that Americans especially have supported this heterodox idea; alas! there is no need to go as far as Boston to encounter the heresy in question. Even here it attacks and breaches true poetry every day. Poetry, if only one is willing to seek within himself, to question his heart, to recall his memories of enthusiasm, has no other goal than itself; it cannot have any other, and no poem will be so great, so noble, so truly worthy of the name of poetry as that which will have been written solely for the pleasure of writing a poem.

I do not mean that poetry does not ennoble manners, —let there be no mistake about it,—that its final result is not to raise man above the level of vulgar interests; that would obviously be an absurdity. I say that, if the poet has pursued a moral aim, he has diminished his poetic force; and it is not rash to wager that his work will be bad. Poetry cannot, under penalty of death or failure, be assimilated to science or morality; it does not have Truth as its object, it has only Itself. The means for demonstrating truth are other and are elsewhere. Truth has nothing to do with songs. All that constitutes the grace, the charm, the irresistible attraction of a song, would take from Truth its authority and its power. Cold, calm, impassive, the demonstrative mood rejects the diamonds and the flowers of the Muse; it is then absolutely the inverse of the poetic mood.

Pure Intellect aims at truth, Taste reveals Beauty, and Moral sense teaches us what is Right. It is true that taste is intimately connected with the other two, and is separated from Moral sense only by so slight a difference that Aristotle has not hesitated to include among the virtues some of its delicate operations. Thus, what especially exasperates the man of taste in the spectacle of vice is its deformity, its disproportion. Vice injures the just and the true, revolts the intellect and the conscience; but, as an outrage to harmony, as dissonance, it will wound more particularly certain poetic minds; and I do not think it scandalous to consider every offense against morality, against moral beauty, as a kind of offense against universal rhythm and prosody.

It is this admirable, this immortal instinct of the beautiful which makes us consider the earth and its spectacles as a revelation, as something in correspondence with Heaven. The insatiable thirst for everything that lies beyond, and that life reveals, is the most living proof of our immortality.

It is at the same time by poetry and *through* poetry, by and *through* music that the soul glimpses the splendors beyond the tomb; and when an exquisite poem brings us to the verge of tears, those tears are not the proof of excessive pleasure; they are rather evidence of an aroused melancholy, of a condition of nerves, of a nature which has been exiled amid the imperfect and which would like to take possession immediately, on this very earth, of a revealed paradise.

Thus, the principle of poetry is precisely and simply human aspiration toward a superior beauty, and the manifestation of this principle is in an enthusiasm, an excitation of the soul,—an enthusiasm altogether independent of passion which is the intoxication of the heart, and of truth which is the food of reason. For passion is *natural,* too natural not to introduce an offensive, discordant tone into the domain of pure beauty, too familiar and too violent not to scandalize the pure Desires, the gracious Melancholies and the noble Despairs which inhabit the supernatural regions of poetry.

This extraordinary elevation, this exquisite delicacy, this accent of immortality which Edgar Poe demands of the Muse, far from making him less attentive to the technique of execution, have impelled him constantly to sharpen his genius as a technician. Many people, especially those who have read the strange poem called *The Raven,* would be shocked if I analyzed the article in which our poet, apparently innocently, but with a slight impertinence which I cannot condemn, has explained in detail the method of construction which he used, the adaptation of the rhythm, the choice of a refrain,—the shortest possible and the most suitable to a variety of applications, and at the same time the most representative of melancholy and despair, embellished with the most sonorous rime of all (nevermore),—the choice of a bird capable of imitating the human voice, but a bird—the raven—branded with a baneful and fatal character in popular imagination,—the choice of the most poetic of all tones, the melancholy tone,—of the most poetic sentiment, love for one dead, etc.—"And I shall not place the hero of my poem in poor surroundings," he says, "because poverty is commonplace and contrary to the idea of Beauty. His melancholy will be sheltered by a magnificently and poetically furnished room."[6] The reader will detect in several of Poe's short stories curious symptoms of this inordinate taste for beautiful forms, especially for beautiful forms that are strange, for ornate surroundings and oriental sumptuousness.

I said that this article seemed marred by a slight impertinence. Confirmed advocates of inspiration would be sure to find in it blasphemy and profanation; but I believe that it is for them especially that the article has been written. Just as certain writers feign carelessness, aiming at a masterpiece with their eyes closed, full of confidence in disorder, expecting that words thrown at the ceiling will fall back on the floor in the form of a poem, so Edgar Poe,—one of the most inspired men I know,—has made a pretense of hiding spontaneity, of simulating coolness and deliberation. "It will not be regarded as a breach of decorum on my part"—he says with an amusing pride which I do not consider in bad taste,—"to show that no one point in its composition is referible either to accident or intuition —that the work proceeded, step by step, to its completion with the precision and rigid consequence of a mathematical problem."[7] Only lovers of chance, I say, only fatalists of inspiration and fanatics of *free verse* can find this *attention to detail* odd. There are no insignificant details in matters of art.

As for free verse, I shall add that Poe attached an

extreme importance to rime, and that in the analysis which he has made of the mathematical and musical pleasure which the mind derives from rime, he has introduced as much care, as much subtlety as in all the other subjects pertaining to the art of poetry. Just as he has shown that the refrain is capable of infinitely varied applications, so also he has sought to renew, to redouble the pleasure derived from rime by adding to it an unexpected element, *the strange,* which is the indispensable condiment, as it were, of all beauty. He often makes a happy use of repetitions of the same line or of several lines, insistent reiterations of phrases which simulate the obsessions of melancholy or of a fixed idea,—of a pure and simple refrain introduced in several different ways,—of a variant-refrain which feigns carelessness and inadvertence,—of rimes redoubled and tripled, and also of a kind of rime which introduces into modern poetry, but with more precision and purpose, the surprises of Leonine verse.

It is obvious that the value of all these means can be proved only through application; and a translation of poetry so studied, so concentrated, can be a fond dream, but only a dream. Poe wrote little poetry; he has sometimes expressed regret at not being able to devote himself, not more often, but exclusively, to this type of work which he considered the most noble. But his poetry always creates a powerful effect. It is not the ardent outpouring of Byron, it is not the soft, harmonious, distinguished melancholy of Tennyson for whom, it may be said in passing, he had an almost fraternal admiration. It is something profound and shimmering like a dream, mysterious and perfect like crystal. I do not need to add, I presume, that American critics have often disparaged his poetry; very recently I found in a dictionary of American biography an article in which it was adjudged esoteric, in which it was feared that this muse in learned garb might create a school in the proud country of utilitarian morality, and in which regret was expressed that Poe had not applied his talents to the expression of moral truths in place of spending them in quest of a bizarre ideal, of lavishing in his verses a mysterious, but sensual voluptuousness.

We are well acquainted with that kind of sparring. The reproaches that bad critics heap upon good poets are the same in all countries. In reading this article it seemed to me that I was reading the translation of one of these numerous indictments brought by Parisian critics against those of our poets who are most fond of perfection. Our favorites are easy to guess and every lover of pure poetry will understand me when I say that among our anti-poetic race Victor Hugo would be less admired if he were perfect, and he has succeeded in having all his lyric genius forgiven only by introducing forcibly and brutually into his poetry what Edgar Poe considered the major modern heresy,—*the teaching of a lesson.*

THE RAVEN, by MANET

BOSTON MUSEUM OF FINE ARTS

Critical Miscellany

1. PREFACE TO MESMERIC REVELATION

Edgar Poe has been much discussed recently, and he deserves to be. With a volume of short stories his reputation has reached across the sea. He has caused astonishment, most of all astonishment, rather than emotion or enthusiasm. That is usually the case with all writers who depend on a method which they themselves have created and which is the natural expression of their temperament. I do not believe that it is possible to find any able writer who has not created his own method, or rather whose native sensibility has not been reflected and transformed into a genuine art. Forceful writers are also apt to be philosophers to a greater or lesser extent: Diderot, Laclos, Hoffmann, Goethe, Jean-Paul, Maturin, Honoré de Balzac, Edgar Poe. Notice that I am taking literary men of every complexion, and the most opposite, as examples. That is true of all of them, even of Diderot, the most audacious and the most adventurous, who applied himself to observe and to control his inspiration, who began by accepting and ended by making a deliberate use of his own enthusiastic, sanguine and boisterous nature. Consider Sterne, whose case is obviously quite different and also quite admirable in a different way. The man made his own method. All these individuals, with tireless effort and good will, interpret nature, pure nature.—Which nature?—Their own. Thus they are usually much more surprising and original than those who simply possess imagination, but completely lack the philosophic spirit, and who line up and pile up events without classifying them and without explaining their mysterious meaning. I have said that they were astonishing. I am going to go further and say that they usually aim at astonishment. In the works of several of these men there can be seen a preoccupation with a perpetual supernaturalism. As I have said, that comes from an inherent tendency *to seek,* from the inquisitive mind, the judicial mind, which perhaps has its roots in the most remote impressions of childhood. Others, determined naturalists, examine the soul with a magnifying glass, as doctors examine the body, and wear out their eyes looking for the hidden spring. Others, of a mixed type, try to fuse these two systems into a mysterious unity. Animal unity, the unity of a universal fluid, the unity of matter, all these recent theories, by a strange coincidence, have somehow entered the minds of poets at the same time that they have entered the minds of scientists.

Thus, finally, there always comes a moment when writers of the type I have been describing become jealous of philosophers, as it were, and then they also set forth their own system of natural philosophy, sometimes even with a certain lack of modesty which has its ingenuousness and its charm. Everyone knows *Séraphitus, Louis Lambert,* and a multitude of passages in other books in which Balzac, a great mind devoured by a legitimate encyclopedic pride, has attempted to harmonize in a unified and definitive system different ideas drawn from Swedenborg, Mesmer, Marat, Goethe and

Geoffroy Saint-Hilaire. Edgar Poe was also absorbed by the idea of unity, and he expended as much effort as Balzac on that fond dream. It is certain that when specifically literary minds put themselves to it, they make strange excursions through philosophy. They cut abrupt openings and see sudden vistas on paths which are entirely theirs.

To summarize, I shall say that the three characteristics of *curious* writers are: 1. a *personal* method; 2. *surprise;* 3. a philosophic mania, three characteristics, moreover, which establish their superiority as writers. The selection from Edgar Poe which follows is sometimes based on excessively tenuous reasoning, in other places it is obscure, and now and then it is exceptionally audacious. It is necessary to make the best of it and to digest it just as it is. Above all it is necessary to follow the text literally. Certain things would have become even more obscure, had I chosen to paraphrase the author, instead of holding myself strictly to the letter. I have preferred to use a painful and sometimes baroque French and to present Edgar Poe's philosophical method in all its truth.

It goes without saying that *La Liberté de penser*[1] cannot be held responsible for the ideas of the American storyteller, and that it simply believed it could please its readers by offering them this highly interesting scientific curiosity.

2. PREFACE TO BERENICE

The story offered to our readers is taken from the works of Edgar Allan Poe. It was one of his first literary productions. Edgar Poe, who could be considered the most notable writer in the United States, died in 1849, at the age of thirty-seven. In effect, he died in the gutter; one morning the police picked him up and took him to a hospital in Baltimore; he departed like Hoffmann and Balzac and so many others, just when he was beginning to be master of his fate. To be perfectly fair, it is necessary to place part of the blame for his vices, and especially his drunkenness, on the Puritanical society in which he was imprisoned by Providence.

Whenever Poe was happy and more or less untroubled, he was the most amiable and the most charming of men. This eccentric and stormy writer had no real consolation in life except the angelic devotion of his mother-in-law, Mrs. Clemm, to whom all solitary hearts will pay a well-deserved homage.

Edgar Poe is not exclusively a poet and a storyteller; he is poet, storyteller and philosopher. He is at the same time both a visionary and a scholar. That he produced a few bad and hastily composed works is not at all surprising; that is explained by his terrible life. But what will always make him worthy of praise is his preoccupation with all the truly important subjects, and those which are *alone* worthy of the attention of a *spiritual* man: probabilities, mental illnesses, scientific hypotheses, hopes and considerations about a future life, analysis of the eccentrics and pariahs of this world, directly symbolic buffooneries. Add to this ceaseless and active ambition of his thought an exceptional erudition, an *astonishing* impartiality which is *antithetical* to his *subjective* nature, an extraordinary power of analysis and deduction, and the customary *tautness* of his writing,—and it will not seem surprising that we have called him the *outstanding figure* of his country. A stubborn attachment to utility, or rather a determined curiosity, distinguishes Poe from all the European romantics, or if you prefer, from all the sectarians of the so-called romantic school.

Poe has been known here previously only by *The Gold Bug, The Black Cat* and *The Murders in the Rue Morgue,* translated in a clear and straightforward manner by Mme. Isabelle Meunier, and by *Mesmeric Revelation,* translated in *Liberté de penser* by Charles Baudelaire, who has just published in the two most recent issues of the *Revue de Paris* a very clear account of the life and general character of the unfortunate Poe and his works. We are obliged to the former for the story which follows.[2]

Poe's principal works are: *Tales of the Grotesque and Arabesque,* which could be translated *Grotesques et Arabesques,* a volume of stories published by Wiley and Putnam in New York; a volume of poetry, *The Literati, Eureka, Arthur Gordon Pym,* and a considerable number of very penetrating critical articles about English and American writers.

3. PREFACE TO THE PHILOSOPHY OF FURNITURE

Who of us, in long hours of leisure, has not found it a delightful pleasure to construct in imagination a model apartment, an ideal home, a *place of dreams?* Guided by his own temperament, everyone has combined silk and gold, wood and metal, has softened the sunlight, or increased the artificial brilliance of lamps, has even invented new forms of furniture, or accumulated old ones.

The article which we are presenting to our readers is by a great American writer, unknown in France, and somewhat misunderstood in the United States. Edgar Poe lived a sad life, and his death was even more sad. Some of his compatriots speak of him only with a certain bitterness, since the young colossus called America has in fact a very thin skin, and even in the smallest matters, finds it hard to tolerate jests. Fenimore Cooper felt that fact very strongly. Cruel remarks such as: *The Yankees alone are preposterous;—we have been brought to merge in simple show our notions of taste itself—the cost of an article of furniture has at length come to be, with us, nearly the whole test of its merit;—the corruption of taste is a portion or a pendant of the dollar-manufacture;*—and sarcastic jokes about the craze for mirrors, for cut glass, and for gas lights in aristocratic American homes,—are certainly hard for a young *parvenu* nation with a delicate throat to swallow.

Impartial or not, this article[3] seemed to us an interesting curiosity, and it will amuse our readers. As for Edgar Poe's personal ideas about furniture, which incidentally seem to us very sensible, they may make what they wish of them. Nevertheless, we cannot help smiling when we see our author, dominated by his almost oriental imagination, fall somewhat into the error for which he reproaches his fellow citizens, and that the room which he offers us as a model of simplicity, is one which will seem to many a model of luxury.

4. PREFACE TO THE RAVEN

THE GENESIS OF A POEM

It has been said that poetics is derived and developed from the study of poems. Here is a poet who claims that his poem was composed in accordance with his poetics. He certainly had great genius and more inspiration than anyone else, if by inspiration is understood energy, intellectual enthusiasm, and the ability to keep one's faculties alert. But he also loved work more than anyone else; he was fond of repeating, he who had a mature originality, that originality is a matter of apprenticeship, which does not mean something that can be transmitted by instruction. The accidental and the unintelligible were his two great enemies. Did he make himself, by a strange and amusing vanity, much less inspired than he naturally was? Did he diminish the spontaneous faculty in himself in order to give will a larger share? I should be rather inclined to think so; although at the same time it must not be forgotten that his genius, however ardent and supple it may have been, was passionately fond of analysis, combinations and calculations. Still another of his favorite axioms was this one: "Everything in a poem or a novel, as in a sonnet or a short story, should lead to the conclusion. A good writer already has his last line in mind when he writes the first one." Thanks to this admirable method, the artist can begin his composition at the end, and work on any part whenever it is convenient. The lovers of a *fine frenzy* will perhaps be revolted by these *cynical* maxims; but everyone may take what he wishes from them. It will always be useful to show them what profit art can draw from deliberation, and to make worldly people realize how much labor is required by that object of luxury called Poetry.

After all, a little charlatanism is always permitted to genius, and is even proper to it. It is, like rouge on the cheeks of a naturally beautiful woman, an additional stimulus to the mind.

Poem strange above all others. It revolves on a profound and mysterious word, as terrible as infinity, that thousands of contorted lips have repeated since the beginning of time, and that in an idle gesture of despair more than one dreamer has written on the corner of his table in order to try out his pen: *Nevermore!* Immensity, made fruitful by destruction, is filled from top to bottom with this idea, and Humanity, still not brutualized, gladly accepts Hell in order to escape the helpless despair contained in that word.

In casting poetry in the form of prose, there is necessarily a dreadful imperfection; but the result would be even worse in a rimed aping of the original. The reader will understand that it is impossible for me to give him an exact idea of the profound and lugubrious sonority, of the powerful monotony of these verses, whose broad and tripled rimes sound like the tolling of melancholy. It is indeed the poem of the sleeplessness of despair; it lacks nothing: neither the fever of ideas, nor the violence of colors, nor sickly reasoning, nor drivelling terror, nor even the bizarre gaiety of suffering which makes it more terrible. Listen to Lamartine's most plaintive stanzas singing in your memory, the most complicated and the most magnificent rhythms of Victor Hugo; mingle with them the recollection of Théophile Gautier's most subtle and most comprehensive tercets,—from *Ténèbres*, for instance, that garland of formidable conceits on death and nothingness, in which the tripled rime adapts itself so well to the obsessive melancholy,—and you will perhaps get an approximate idea of Poe's talents as a versifier; I say as versifier, for it is superflous, I believe, to speak of his imagination.

But I hear the reader murmuring like Alcestis: "We shall see!"—Here is the poem.[4]

5. POSTSCRIPT TO HANS PFAALL

The Unparalleled Adventure of One Hans Pfaall was first published in the *Southern Literary Messenger*, the first literary magazine edited by Poe in Richmond. He was then twenty-three years old. In the posthumous edition of his works,—which by the way is far from being complete—a very strange postscript appears at the end of *Hans Pfaall*[5] which I wish to analyze, and which will show the reader that this publication involved one of the childish aspects of this great genius.

Poe discusses different works all of which have the same purpose,—a trip to the moon, a description of the moon, etc. . . . mystifications, or,—as Americans, who like so much to be fooled, call them,—hoaxes. Poe takes pains to show how inferior these works are to his own, because they lack the most important characteristic—one which I shall explain presently.

He begins by citing the *Moon Story* or *Moon Hoax* by Mr. Locke, which, I presume, is the same unfortunate *Animaux dans la lune* which about twenty years ago caused some stir on our old continent, already too Americanized. He begins, first of all, by establishing the fact that his *literary stunt* was published in the *Southern Literary Messenger* three weeks before Locke published his *hoax* in the *New York Sun*. Several papers collated the two works and published them simultaneously, and Poe quite rightly expresses his resentment at that imposed relationship.

For the public to have *swallowed* Locke's *Moon Hoax,* an improbable degree of astronomical ignorance would have been required.

Locke's telescope is not sufficiently powerful to enable Herschel, the hero of the *hoax,* to see animals and flowers on the moon, and to distinguish the forms of birds and the color of their eyes, at a distance of 240,000 miles from the earth. Finally, the lenses of his telescope were made by Hartley and Grant; now, says Poe in a triumphant manner, these gentlemen went out of business several years before the publication of the hoax.

With regard to a kind of hairy veil which shades the eyes of lunar bison, Herschel (Locke) claims that it was provided by nature in order to protect the animal's eyes against the violent alternation of light and shadow to which are subjected all creatures living on the side of the moon facing the earth. But this alternation does not exist; the inhabitants, if there are any, cannot experience darkness. Lacking the sun, they are lighted by the earth.

His lunar topography *puts the heart on the right side,* so to speak. It contradicts all the maps and is self-contradictory. The author does not realize that on a lunar map the east should be to the left.

Deceived by the vague names such as *Mare Nubium, Mare Tranquillitatis, Mare Fecunditatis,* which ancient astronomers gave to the spots on the moon, Locke goes into details about the seas and liquid masses of the moon. Now, it is an established astronomical fact that there are none.

The description of the wings of his *man-bat* is plagiarized from the *flying islanders* of Peter Wilkins. Somewhere Locks says: "What a prodigious influence must our thirteen times larger globe have exercised upon this satellite when an embryo in the womb of time, the passive subject of chemical affinity!" That is quite sublime; but an astronomer would not have said it, and above all he would not have written it in a scientific journal published in Edinburgh. For astronomers know that the earth,—in the sense indicated by the above phrase,—is not thirteen times, but forty-nine times as large as the moon.

And here is a remark which shows Poe's analytical mind quite well. "How distinctly Herschel sees animals," he says, "how minutely he describes their forms and colors!" That is false observation! As a fabricator of hoaxes he does not know his job. For what is the thing that immediately and above all would strike and impress a *real* observer, if he should see animals on the moon,—even though he might have been able to foresee it:—"They would appear to be walking, with heels up and head down, in the manner of flies on a ceiling!" —That shows a true sense of nature.

The conceptions about vegetables and animals are not based on analogy; the wings of the *man-bat* are insufficient to support him in an atmosphere as rarefied as that of the moon;—"the transfusion of artifical light through the focal object of vision" is pure nonsense;— if it were only a question of making lenses strong enough to see what is happening on a planet, man might succeed, but the celestial body would have to have enough light, and the more distant it is, the more diffused is the light, etc.

This is Poe's conclusion, which is rather interesting for those who like to investigate the workroom of a man of genius,—Jean-Paul's square sheets of paper strung together on pieces of cord,—Balzac's tangled proofs,—Buffon's marginal notes, etc. . . .

> In these various *brochures* the aim is always satirical; the theme being a description of Lunarian customs as compared with ours. In none is there any effort at *plausibility* in the details of the voyage itself. The writers seem, in each instance, to be utterly uninformed in respect to astronomy. In "Hans Pfaall" the design is original, inasmuch as regards an attempt at *verisimilitude*, in the application of scientific principles (so far as the whimsical nature of the subject would permit), to the actual passage between the earth and the moon.

The reader may smile,—discovering Poe's juvenile *fetishes* [*dadas*], I have smiled more than once myself. Will not the petty aspects of the great always be a touching spectacle for an impartial mind? It is truly strange to see a mind sometimes so profoundly Germanic and sometimes so deeply Oriental, betray on occasion the Americanism with which it is saturated.

But, in spite of all that, admiration prevails. Who may I ask, who among us,—I am speaking of the most hardy,—would have dared at the age of twenty-three, at the age when one learns to *read*,—to take off for the moon, adequately equipped with astronomical and scientific notions, and to ride imperturably the *hobbyhorse* [*dada*] or rather the capricious hippogriff of *verisimilitude?*

6. ORIGINAL DEDICATION TO MRS. CLEMM

To Mrs. Maria Clemm

Milford, Connecticut, United States of America

For a long time, Madam, I have wished to please you by this translation[6] of one of the greatest poets of this century; but literary life is full of vicissitudes and stumbling blocks, and I am afraid that Germany may precede me in the accomplishment of this pious homage owed to the memory of a writer who, like the Hoffmanns, the Jean-Pauls, the Balzacs, is less of his own country than he is of the world. Two years before the catastrophe which horribly destroyed his life, so full and so ardent, I had already undertaken to introduce Edgar Poe to the literary public of my country. But at that time his ever stormy life was unknown to me; I did not know that those dazzling growths were the product of a volcanic soil, and when today I compare the false idea which I had formed of his life with the reality,—the Edgar Poe created by my imagination,—rich, happy,—a young gentleman of genius who sometimes turned his hand to literature in the midst of the countless activities of an elegant life,—when I compare that with the true Edgar,—poor Eddie, whom you loved and succored, whom I shall make known in France,—the ironic antithesis fills me with an inescapable compassion. Several years have passed, and I have been constantly obsessed by his ghost. Today, I am not only delighted to present his beautiful stories, but also to inscribe above them the name of the woman who was always so gentle and kind to him. As you bound his wounds with your love, so he will preserve your name with his glory.

You will read what I have said about his life and works; you will tell me whether I have properly understood his character, his sufferings and the special quality of his mind—and, if I am wrong, you will correct me. If passion has led me into error, you may redress the balance. Whatever you say, Madam, will be heard with respect and gratitude, even any slight resentment you may feel as a result of my severity toward your fellow Americans, which was doubtless the result of a need to relieve the feeling of hatred aroused in my free soul by commercial and physiocratic societies.

I owe this public homage to a mother whose greatness and goodness honor the World of Letters as much as the marvelous creations of her son. I should be inexpressibly happy if an errant ray of that benevolence which was the sun of his life could, across the sea that separates us, reach me, insignificant and obscure,[7] and comfort me with its magnetic warmth.

Goodbye, Madam; among the various salutations and complimentary formulas which may conclude a letter from one *soul* to another *soul,* I know only one that corresponds with the feelings which you inspire in me: Goodness, goddess.

7. TRANSLATOR'S NOTE

To those who sincerely appreciate the talents of Edgar Poe I shall say that I consider my task finished,[8] although, for their sake, it would have been a pleasure for me to continue. The two volumes of *Histoires Extraordinaires* and *Nouvelles Histoires Extraordinaires* and the *Aventures d'Arthur Gordon Pym* are sufficient to present Edgar Poe in his various aspects as a visionary teller of tales now terrible, now gracious, in turn mocking and tender, always a philosopher and analyst, a lover of the magic of absolute verisimilitude, a lover of the most detached buffoonery. *Eureka* revealed a subtle and ambitious dialectician. If my task could be continued fruitfully in a country such as France, it would remain for me to present Edgar Poe as a poet and Edgar Poe as a literary critic. Every true lover of poetry will recognize that the first of these duties is very nearly an impossibility, and that my very humble and very devoted skill as translator is insufficient to make up for the missing pleasures of rhythm and rime. For those who are very sensitive, all the marvels of the pure poet can be at least partly glimpsed through the fragments of poetry included in the stories, such as the *Conqueror Worm* in *Ligeia*, the *Haunted Palace* in *The Fall of the House of Usher* and the so mysteriously eloquent poem called *The Raven.*

As for the second kind of talent, criticism, it is easy to understand that what I could call Edgar Poe's *Monday Chats*[9] would have little chance of pleasing light-minded Parisians, very little concerned with the literary quarrels which divide a still young country, and which, in literature as in politics, make the North an enemy of the South.

In conclusion, I may say to Edgar Poe's unknown French friends that I am proud and happy to have introduced them to a new kind of beauty; and also, why should I not admit that what sustained my will was the pleasure of presenting to them a man who resembled me somewhat, in certain respects, that is to say a part of myself?

I am justified in believing that very soon the editors of the popular edition of Edgar Poe's works will feel the glorious necessity of publishing them in a more substantial way, in a form more suitable for the libraries of booklovers, and in an edition in which the component parts will be definitively and more appropriately grouped.

APPENDIX

LIST OF POE'S WORKS TRANSLATED BY BAUDELAIRE

1856 *Histoires Extraordinaires*, published in Paris by Michel Lévy.

To My Mother [which was used in his dedication to Maria Clemm]. The Murders in the Rue Morgue — The Purloined Letter — The Gold Bug—The Balloon Hoax—The Unparalleled Adventure of One Hans Pfaall—MS. Found in a Bottle—A Descent Into the Maelström—The Facts in the Case of M. Valdemar —Mesmeric Revelation—A Tale of the Ragged Mountains—Morella — Ligeia — Metzengerstein

1857 *Nouvelles Histoires Extraordinaires,* published in Paris by Michel Lévy.

The Imp of the Perverse—The Black Cat—William Wilson—The Man of the Crowd—The Tell-Tale Heart—Berenice—The Fall of the House of Usher—The Pit and the Pendulum—Hop-Frog—The Cask of Amontillado—The Masque of the Red Death—King Pest—The Devil in the Belfry—Lionizing—Four Beasts in One—Some Words with a Mummy —The Power of Words—The Colloquy of Monos and Una—The Conversation of Eiros

and Charmion—Shadow-A Parable—Silence-A Fable—The Island of the Fay—The Oval Portrait

1858 *Aventures d'Arthur Gordon Pym,* published in Paris by Michel Lévy.

1863 *Eureka,* published in Paris by Michel Lévy.

1865 *Histoires Grotesques Et Sérieuses,* published in Paris by Michel Lévy.

The Mystery of Marie Rogêt—Maelzel's Chess Player—Eleanora—A Tale of Jerusalem—The Angel of the Odd—The System of Doctor Tarr and Professor Fether—The Domain of Arnheim—Landor's Cottage—The Philosophy of Furniture—The Raven [previously published in magazines, for the first time in 1853] —The Philosophy of Composition

NOTES

INTRODUCTION

1. See Rémy de Gourmont, *Promenades littéraires,* Paris, Mercure de France, 1904.
2. *Literary History of the United States,* ed. Robert E. Spiller et al; New York, 1948, v. 3, p. 691.
3. Professor W. T. Bandy has discovered a French adaptation of Poe's *William Wilson* published in France in 1844, i.e., before the Wiley and Putnam edition appeared (information furnished in a letter).
4. Most of the quotations are taken from letters and whenever possible reference will be made simply to the number of the letter in Crépet's volumes devoted to *Correspondance Générale.* The letter to Fraisse is number 502 (III, p. 41).
5. *Correspondance Générale,* letter number 134 (I, p. 195).
6. See the Christopher Isherwood translation of Baudelaire's *Intimate Journals,* Hollywood, Marcel Rodd, 1947, p. 107.
7. See Jacques Crépet, *Oeuvres Posthumes,* Paris, Louis Conard, 1939, p. 570. This is volume 11 of *Oeuvres Complètes de Charles Baudelaire.* Unless otherwise specified, all references are to Jacques Crépet's edition of Baudelaire's work.
8. *Ibid.,* p. 574.
9. *Correspondance Générale,* letter 122 (I, pp. 160-161).
10. *Ibid.,* letter 231 (I, p. 378).
11. *Les Paradis Artificiels, opium et haschisch,* a work in prose by Baudelaire, was based on De Quincey's *Confessions of an English Opium Eater* as well as on his own experience.
12. Baudelaire used this word in his article on the painting exhibition, *Exposition Universelle de 1855.* See Crépet, *Curiosités Esthétiques,* p. 235.
13. See Alfred H. Barr, Jr., *Fantastic Art, Dada, Surrealism,* 3rd ed., New York, Museum of Modern Art, 1946, p. 53 and p. 60.
14. *Correspondance Générale,* letter 234 (I, p. 381).

15. Quoted from Marcel Raymond, *From Baudelaire to Surrealism*, New York, Wittenborn and Schultz, 1950, p. 17. Translated by G. M.
16. In addition to being a poet and literary critic, Baudelaire was a distinguished art critic. Most of his articles in that field were published the year after his death under the title *Curiosités Esthétiques.*
17. *Correspondance Générale,* letter 235 (I, p. 386).
18. From Champfleury, *Souvenirs et Portraits,* Paris, 1863, p. 142. Quoted by Crépet in *Histoires Extraordinaires,* p. 353.
19. See Campbell Dodgson, *Albrecht Dürer,* London and Boston, The Medici Society, 1926, p. 51; and Daniel C. Rich, *Seurat and the Evolution of "La Grande Jatte,"* Chicago, University of Chicago Press, 1935, p. 35.
20. The despair and contempt behind Dadaism, expressing themselves in shock tactics, are only more recent examples of psychological phenomena observable in Baudelaire and other rebellious nineteenth century artists. See Barr, *Fantastic Art, Dada, Surrealism.*
21. Crépet, *Histoires Extraordinaires,* p. 293.
22. Crépet, *Histoires Grotesques et Sérieuses,* pp. 239-240.
23. *Correspondance Générale,* letter 170 (I, p. 266).
24. *Ibid.,* letter 844 (IV, p. 277).
25. This essay appears in *Variété II,* Paris, Librairie Gallimard, 1930.
26. For the artists mentioned, see the following publications: John Rewald, *Gauguin,* Paris and New York, Hyperion Press, 1938, p. 119; Carl Zigrosser, *The Book of Fine Prints,* New York, Crown Publishers, 1948, p. 154; *Life Magazine,* February 26, 1951: information to be published by Lloyd Goodrich in his forthcoming book on Ryder; Florent Fels, *James Ensor,* Geneva and Brussels, Editions Pierre Cailler, 1947, p. 53; *Paul Klee,* New York, Museum of Modern Art Catalogue, 1941, p. 4; Marcel Guérin, *L'Oeuvre Gravé de Manet,* Paris, Librairie Floury, 1944, pp. 84 ff.
27. Quoted from Marcel Raymond, *From Baudelaire to Surrealism,* p. 18.
28. *Correspondance Générale,* letter 233 (I, 380).

1852—EDGAR ALLAN POE, HIS LIFE AND WORKS

1. The Goncourt brothers, in their *Journal,* mention a convict thus tattooed. Crépet, 11, p. 568.
2. Vauvenargues was a French moralist of the eighteenth century whose *Maxims* are less pessimistic than those of La Rochefoucauld.
3. *Leur chien même les mord et leur donne la rage.*
   Un ami jurera qu'ils ont trahi le roi.
   These lines are from Théophile Gautier's poem *Ténèbres.*
4. The reference is to Alfred de Vigny's book *Stello,* which was published in 1832.
5. The biographer in question was P. Pendleton Cooke who wrote an article on Poe in the *Southern Literary Messenger* in 1848.
6. The unnamed critic was perhaps James Russell Lowell who had written about Poe in *Graham's Magazine* in 1845.
7. There was no legal adoption. It seems to have been Mrs. Allan who was interested in the child.
8. Poe's works are full of French phrases. [Baudelaire's note.]
9. Poe's life, his adventures in Russia and his correspondence have long been promised by American magazines, but have never appeared. C.B. [Baudelaire's note.]
10. The prize winning story was *MS. Found in a Bottle,* for which he received $50.00.
11. Poe was forty years old at the time of his death.
12. Poe's friend, the writer Nathaniel P. Willis, wrote an obituary notice which appeared in the *Home Journal* on the Saturday following Poe's death. It was reprinted by Griswold and later biographers.
13. Baudelaire wrote a poem in imitation of Longfellow which is entitled *Le Calumet De Paix* (The Pipe of Peace).
14. Joseph de Maistre was an authoritarian philosopher of the late eighteenth and early nineteenth century. He wrote *Soirées de Saint-Petersbourg.*
15. Baudelaire's source was an article published by P. Pen-

dleton Cooke in the *Southern Literary Messenger* in 1848, from which the following passage is quoted:

> For my individual part, having the seventy or more tales, analytic, mystic, grotesque, arabesque, always wonderful, often great, which his industry and fertility have already given us, I would like to read one cheerful book made by his *invention*, with little or no aid from its twin brother *imagination*—a book in his admirable style of full, minute, never tedious narrative—a book full of homely doings, of successful toils, of ingenious shifts and contrivances, of ruddy firesides—a book healthy and happy throughout, and with no poetry in it at all anywhere, except a good old English 'poetic justice' in the end. Such a book, such as Mr. Poe could make it, would be a book for the million, and if it did nothing to exalt him with the few, would yet certainly *endear* him to them. See Harrison's edition of Poe, I, p. 390.

16. Baudelaire's poem *La Pipe*, reflects the modern addiction to tobacco.
17. *Mesmeric Revelation* was the first of Poe's stories to be translated and published by Baudelaire.
18. The story referred to is *The Conversation of Eiros and Charmion.*
19. The passage quoted is not in the English text. It was either done from memory or was simply meant to summarize the situation.
20. There is no description of the tavern. Again, Baudelaire must have been writing from memory (according to one of his friends he had memorized *The Black Cat)* or was strongly stimulated by Poe's suggestions of the effects of drink.
21. In a letter to Jules Troubat, dated March 5, 1866, Baudelaire wrote:

    > I am very happy to learn of Sainte-Beuve's recovery. I have not had feelings of this sort about the health of others, except in the case of E. Delacroix, who was moreover a great egoist. But affections come to me largely through my mind. Crépet, 11 p. 576.

22. Several of these phrases appear in French in Poe's story:

"Of Mademoiselle Sallé it has been well said: '*Que tous ses pas étaient des sentiments,*' and of Berenice I more seriously believed *que tous ses dents étaient des idées.*"

23. Elsewhere Baudelaire speaks much less favorably of George Sand.
24. Baudelaire published his translation of the *Narrative of Arthur Gordon Pym* in 1858.
25. Baudelaire published a translation of *Eureka* in 1863.
26. Saint-Just was a supporter of Robespierre, with whom he was executed.
27. As the final entry in his *Intimate Journals* Baudelaire wrote:

    I swear henceforth to observe the following rules as the eternal rules of my life: To pray every morning to God, source of all power and all justice; to my father, to Marietta [his old servant] and to Poe as intercessors: to give me the strength necessary to accomplish all my duties . . . . See Isherwood, *Intimate Journals*, p. 112.

1856—EDGAR POE, HIS LIFE AND WORKS

1. *L'aigle, pour le briser, du haut du firmament*
   Sur leur front découvert lâchera la tortue,
   Car ils doivent périr inévitablement
   These lines are from Théophile Gautier's poem *Ténèbres.* There is a legend that an eagle dropped a tortoise on the bald head of the Greek dramatist Aeschylus. Probably Gautier had that story in mind when he was writing these lines. Information furnished by Professor R. E. Dengler.
2. The book was Alfred de Vigny's *Stello.*
3. The biographer was P. Pendleton Cooke. See note 5 in part one.
4. Possibly James Russell Lowell. See note 6 in part one.
5. Nathaniel P. Willis. See note 12 in part one.
6. The reference is to George Sand, about whom he wrote quite bitterly in his *Intimate Journals.*
7. See note 7 in part one.

8. James Russell Lowell used this phrase in his article on Poe, published in *Graham's Magazine* in 1845.
9. See note 10 in part one.
10. Gérard de Nerval, who committed suicide on January 26, 1855. A study of his life by S. A. Rhodes was published by the Philosophical Library on January 26, 1951, the anniversary of his death.
11. Baudelaire raised the question of suicide several times. A newly discovered Baudelaire manuscript, which is an outline of a story to have been called *La Conspiration*, is the most recent evidence of his preoccupation with suicide. The manuscript was published and discussed by Georges Blin in the February, 1951, issue of *Esprit.*
12. Baudelaire has changed the original order of the paragraphs.
13. Poe also believed in phrenology; in reviewing a book on the subject he wrote: "Phrenology is no longer to be laughed at."
14. This passage is a brief foretaste of Proust. René Galand has shown some of the connections between the two writers in his article *Proust et Baudelaire,* published in the December 1950 issue of *PMLA.*
15. It is interesting to note that Baudelaire gave Delacroix a copy of his translations of Poe. The painter enjoyed the stories, but did not relish the comparison.

1857—NEW NOTES ON EDGAR POE

1. The *Diable Amoureux* was written by Jacques Cazotte, who was executed in 1792.
2. This paragraph is from Poe's "Fifty Suggestions." The final quotation—"to deny what is and to explain what is not"—is from Rousseau's *Nouvelle Héloise.*
3. Allamistakeo appears in Poe's *Some Words with a Mummy.*
4. This quotation is from Poe's "Fifty Suggestions."
5. This quotation is likewise from "Fifty Suggestions."
6. Baudelaire published a translation of Poe's article, *The Philosophy of Composition,* in 1859. It is interesting

to compare the few lines quoted here with the corresponding lines in Poe:

> I determined, then, to place the lover in his chamber . . . The room is represented as richly furnished—this in mere pursuance of the ideas I have already explained on the subject of Beauty, as the sole true poetical thesis.

7. This passage is also from *The Philosophy of Composition.*

CRITICAL MISCELLANY

1. *Mesmeric Revelation,* Baudelaire's first Poe translation, was published in the magazine *Liberté de penser* in July, 1848.
2. *Berenice* was first published in *l'Illustration* in April, 1852. Lemonnier has shown that Baudelaire wrote this preface.
3. *The Philosophy of Furniture* was first published in the *Magasin des Familles* in October, 1852.
4. This preface, which precedes Baudelaire's prose translation of *The Raven,* was first published in the *Revue française* in April, 1859.
5. *Hans Pfaall* was first published in *Le Pays* in April, 1855.
6. This original dedication to Mrs. Clemm was published in *Le Pays* in July, 1854. It was followed by the series of translations which later formed the volume entitled *Histoires Extraordinaires,* which appeared in 1856.
7. On a sheet of corrections Baudelaire crossed out this phrase.
8. This text is from a manuscript note probably written about 1860 when Baudelaire was planning a new edition of his translations. The manuscript was first published by M. Y.-G. Le Dantec in 1934, in the *Cahiers Jacques Doucet* and reprinted by M. Jacques Crépet in 1936 in his edition of *Eureka.*
9. The reference is to the *Causeries de lundi* by Saint-Beuve.